Finding Birds ir

Introduction

This is an updated version of my previous book, Fin revolutionary in giving clear maps and directions to pla Laguna de Taraje and the many tracks around the nc updated in 1995 so this new version has been long overdue. Since then there has been an explosion of information available to birdwatchers, not just through the publication of even more books but also through the many trip reports that are available on the internet. However, so much information can be daunting; it can take hours to wade through trip reports ('...and then we went here and the weather was lovely but our car broke down..') to find the gems of information that are really useful or new. And even then, places tend to be described by long descriptions of tracks and turnings instead of clear, simple maps. I'd like to think this book can save you a lot of that work. It presents what I think are the key sites in the area, with the latest information, the clearest maps and my own knowledge that has come from many visits, most recently in 2009 when I visited nearly all the sites in this book.

So, refresh yourself with the latest news of the familiar sites and discover some 'new' ones such as the Cañada de Las Norias, the Lagunas de Espera, Rambla Morales, the Laguna de la Mejorada, the Odiel estuary, La Lantejuela and Cañada de Rianzuela. This book gives you the best advice for finding increasing species such as White-headed Duck, Red-knobbed Coot, Marbled Duck and Black-shouldered Kite, declining birds such as Great Bustard and Black-bellied Sandgrouse and new exotics such as Black-rumped Waxbill.

However, as a book, like all others, it has its limitations. It can't really give you a 'feel' for a place – what it's REALLY like. I've therefore also produced a DVD which is complimentary to the book, showing most of the sites and the birds that were found there on my visit in 2009. This, I hope, gives you an even better idea of what to expect, what the viewing facilities are like, how close you get to the birds and what sounds might help you find the birds you're looking for. In addition there will be further information, and photos, available on our website www.findingbirds.co.uk. Together, I hope the book, the DVD and the website will give you all you need to prepare you for a birding trip to Andalucia.

Good luck,

Dave Gosney, August 2009.

Acknowledgements

My recent trip to Spain was greatly informed by several new books, especially Where to Watch Birds in Spain (Montero, 2006), Where to Watch Birds in Doñana (Moreno and Gutierrez, 2006) and the recently updated Where to Watch Birds in Southern and Western Spain (Garcia and Patterson, 2008) all of which I can thoroughly recommend. I also plundered the internet for trip reports (especially from the excellent www.birdtours.co.uk) and gleaned what information I could from contributions by messrs Barthorpe, Bonser, Bottomley, Cantelo, Crouch, Davies, Djert, Dunn, Easterbook, Eaton, Girdley, Goedelt, Griffiths, Hall, Hodgkin, Jack, Johns, Kinley, Kirschel, Lister, Mason, Miller, Raes, Stidwell, Swann, Thorneycroft, and Wilce (phew!). Thanks too to the numerous people who have written to me with updates to my earlier book, especially Mike Smith and Roger Smith. I'm grateful to Neil Donaghy of Oriole Birding for sending me on 'fam trips' to Spain, organized by Beltran de Ceballos and run by local birders such as Jesus Gallardo Garcia who has been particularly helpful.

Lastly, the person I'm most grateful to is my wife Liz who, despite being a non-birder has launched herself into the travelling, birding, filming, editing and designing with a forbearance way beyond the call of duty.

The Odiel Estuary
(Marismas del Odiel)

Attraction

The Odiel estuary is just 40km from the more famous Coto Doñana and has many of the same birds. However, access here is much easier and excellent views can be had from the road which runs through the heart of the area, making it particularly good for photographers. Special birds include Red-knobbed Coot (probably easier to see here than anywhere else in Europe), Spoonbill (the largest colony in Spain) and Osprey (one of only a very few pairs in mainland Spain breeds within sight of the road).

Getting there

The best birding sites are on the west bank of the Odiel river, opposite Huelva. From Huelva, take the A-497 (A492) towards Punta Umbria and Ayamonte. Immediately after crossing the Odiel river, turn left to a roundabout where the turning to 'Marismas del Odiel' is signposted. Follow this road through the reserve.

Notes

1. The area to the east of the road is a saltmarsh (37.26410N 6.98059W). Montagu's Harriers are a particular attraction; we had two males and two females in late March, behaving as if they would breed here, though it's possible they were just coming to roost.

2. Look out for a little lane to the east (37.25418N 6.96941W) to a restaurant called La Calatilla. North of this lane is an area of open water created by gravel pit-like excavations (referred to in some trip reports as Laguna la Batusca). This pool is good for waders and ducks (especially Shoveler, Gadwall and Red-crested Pochard) but it is also a breeding site for Red-knobbed Coot. In 2009 there were two pairs, one with a nest, in the rushes immediately adjacent to the restaurant road, giving fantastic views. One of them had a white collar indicating that it had been released as part of the breeding program on the Coto Doñana. I don't know any other site in Europe where this species can be seen so reliably and at such close range.

3. On the south side of the restaurant road is another, smaller, pool, with a more extensive marshy surround. This is overlooked by a lovely hide from which the views are excellent. In late March we had stilts, redshanks, snipe, Shoveler, egrets and Spoonbill and heard Red-knobbed Coot. To get to the hide, drive into the car park of the visitor centre (37.25265N 6.96798W) and keep left along the paths between the centre and the restaurant.

4. Opposite the visitor centre are saltpans which are usually populated with flamingoes. These can look particularly spectacular at dusk when the sun is setting behind them.

5. It is possible to walk on either side of the channel to the west of the road. The track along the north side (from 37.25143N 6.96883W) leads to a point overlooking the Spoonbill colony (up to 500 pairs have bred here, making this the biggest colony in Iberia). However, the views from this point are not worth making a trek for – you'll see them much closer elsewhere. Instead, look out for estuarine waders in the creek, flamingos in the saltpans and Ospreys fishing along the channel. Up to a dozen Ospreys winter in this area. The track on the south side of the creek leads to a hide (37.24614N 6.96990W) which was pretty useless on my visit in late March.

MARISMAS DEL ODIEL
Area around visitor centre

0 metres 500

N →

Roundabout with signpost to Marismas del Odiel

A492/A497 to Ayamonte and Punta Umbria

Spoonbill colony on this island (500 pairs)

Viewpoint overlooking creek and distant Spoonbills

Another hide — pretty poor in 2009

more saltpans

To coast and causeway (sites 6 and 7)

Visitor centre and car park (P)

La Catalilla restaurant

Rio Odiel

2 bridges to Huelva

Rio Odiel

main A492/A497 road

minor road

saltmarsh

Breeding — or at least roosting — area for Montagu's Harriers

Saltpans particularly good for views of flamingoes

creek popular with fishing Ospreys

Gravel pit for ducks and breeding Red Knobbed Coot (* = nest 2009)

Attractive freshwater pool overlooked by hide (H)

① ④ ④ ② ③ ⑤ H

6. Since 2003, young ospreys from Finland have been released into the wild in two areas of Andalucia, the Alcornocales National Park and here on the Odiel marshes. Possibly as a result of this, breeding has now occurred at both sites (the first in mainland Spain for over 20 years). The pair nesting here at Odiel have chosen a site that is easily visible from the road. After crossing the raised bridge, look out for an open area to the west with a single pylon in the middle – the nest is on that pylon. There's no need to leave the road – if you do you'll be accosted by local conservationists who are protecting these birds.

7. As you drive down the road you will pass close to pools and creeks where you should see plenty of Spoonbills in small groups. Later the road becomes a narrow causeway from which you have views of the river on one side and a saltmarsh on the other. You should get excellent views of waders and terns here (37.161781N 6.91404W) especially if you use your vehicle as a hide. You can follow this road as far as the shore where large numbers of gulls and terns often gather; Audouin's Gulls are usually present and Caspian Terns are regular.

8. Nearby is the Laguna de El Portil (37.21188N 7.04400W) a site which is good for waterfowl including regular White-headed Duck and Ferruginous Duck, especially, but not exclusively, in winter. Purple Heron and Little Bittern occur around the margins. To get there, look for a service road to the right just as you reach El Portal from the east. Park on there and view from the observation platform.

9. The Lagunas de Palos y las Madres are accessed via the road from Huelva to Mazagon. They are said to be good for lake and reedbed species but, in common with some other birders, I failed to locate anywhere worthwhile on a brief visit in 2009. I've since scoured trip reports (and Google Earth!) to try to work out where I went wrong. It seems the best site is the Laguna Primera de Palos where species such as Purple Gallinule and Purple Heron are common and there's a chance of Little Bittern, Savi's Warbler, Moustached Warbler, Penduline Tit, Common Waxbill, Glossy Ibis, Red-crested Pochard and Whiskered Tern. This is also one of the sites where Red-knobbed Coot have been released and can be seen complete with white neck collars. To get there, find a pull-in on the north side of the N-442, immediately east of the big oil refinery, (eg perhaps 37.16999N 6.89455W ie just east of km 11, if there is one). From there, look for a vantage point allowing you to scan over the lake across the railway line.

For details of the other lakes in this group, including notes on where I went wrong, which might prevent you from making the same mistakes, take a look at www.findingbirds.com and look for the section on the Lagunas de Palos y las Madres. The 'comments' facility there will allow you to add any notes of your own that might help others to get the most from this site.

MARISMAS DEL ODIEL
The Odiel Estuary

A472 to Portugal

Best area sites 1-5 see detail overleaf

El Portil ⑧

A497 to Punta Umbria

Laguna de El Portil – for ducks including White-headed

PUNTA UMBRIA

Terrific views of spoonbills, waders and terns from the causeway

HUELVA

A49 to Sevilla

Rio Odiel

Site of Osprey nest – one of the first in mainland Spain

Lagunas de Palos y Las Madres – chance of Little Bittern, White-headed Duck etc

Rio Odiel

N442 to Mazagon

0 — km — 5

N ↑ S

The Coto Doñana
(pronounced Don-yarna)

Attraction

This is one of the most famous birdwatching localities in Europe, a national park of major international importance. On the north-western bank of the Guadalquivir river is a vast area which seasonally floods to produce marshes or marismas, but there are also a number of other lakes and pools as well as vast areas of rice paddies which are often flooded. Amongst the thousands of waterbirds which are attracted here are small numbers of Red-knobbed Coot, Marbled Duck, White-headed Duck, Red-crested Pochard, Ferruginous Duck and Purple Gallinule. A variety of herons and warblers also breed, as do Collared Pratincole, Gull-billed Tern, Pin-tailed Sandgrouse, Red-necked Nightjar, Great Spotted Cuckoo, Azure-winged Magpie and Lesser Short-toed Lark. Birds of prey are exceptionally numerous here including several pairs of Spanish Imperial Eagles and now Black-shouldered Kites too. In winter there are also cranes and Little Bustards. Although the most special parts of the reserve are inaccessible to the public, this book describes a number of sites and routes on the periphery of the reserve where all of these species have been seen, though some of them are elusive.

Getting There

Coming from Sevilla on the A-49/E-01 motorway towards Huelva, after crossing the Guadalquivir river, you can either turn off immediately towards Coria del Rio (and hence Isla Mayor and Venta del Cruce) or come off at junction 23 to reach Villamanrique (via Pilas) or turn south at junction 48 towards El Rocio (via Bollullos). The birding areas can then be reached by following the maps given here.

Access

Most of the Parque Nacional de Doñana is fenced off and inaccessible to the public, unless you take one of the organised excursions to these innermost areas as described under sites 6-9. However, all the other areas are open to the public, though some such as sites 10-16 can only be reached via a very long (almost 50 km) drive on bumpy tracks that can be impassable after heavy rains.

Notes

1. In winter and spring, the area south of El Rocio town is usually flooded, creating what I call 'El Rocio Lagoon' (correct name: La Madre de las Marismas). This area can be viewed from the promenade at El Rocio or from the car park (37.13028N 6.49065W) off the A-483, by the Meson La Choza restaurant (where the light is often better and there are fewer tourists to trouble you). The lagoon can be teeming with herons, egrets, flamingoes, ibis, greylags ducks and waders. Marsh terns, especially Whiskered, are often present in spring and summer when there's also a chance of Gull-billed Tern and Collared Pratincole. Marbled Duck and Little Bittern have been seen here too. Raptors, especially kites and Marsh Harrier, are usually constantly visible and Black-shouldered Kites are sometimes seen at the eastern end of the marsh. With a telescope you might spot eagles or vultures sitting in trees on the far side of the lagoon. Booted and Short-toed Eagles are the most likely but Spanish Imperial Eagle is possible throughout the year and in winter both Lesser Spotted and Spotted Eagle have been reported. Beware that in dry periods the lagoon can become dry and virtually birdless.

2. The information centre of La Rocina is clearly signposted to the west of the road just south of the bridge (turn off at 37.12383N 6.49575W). From the centre, a nature trail takes you 2.5 km upstream from the bridge and includes 4 hides overlooking the

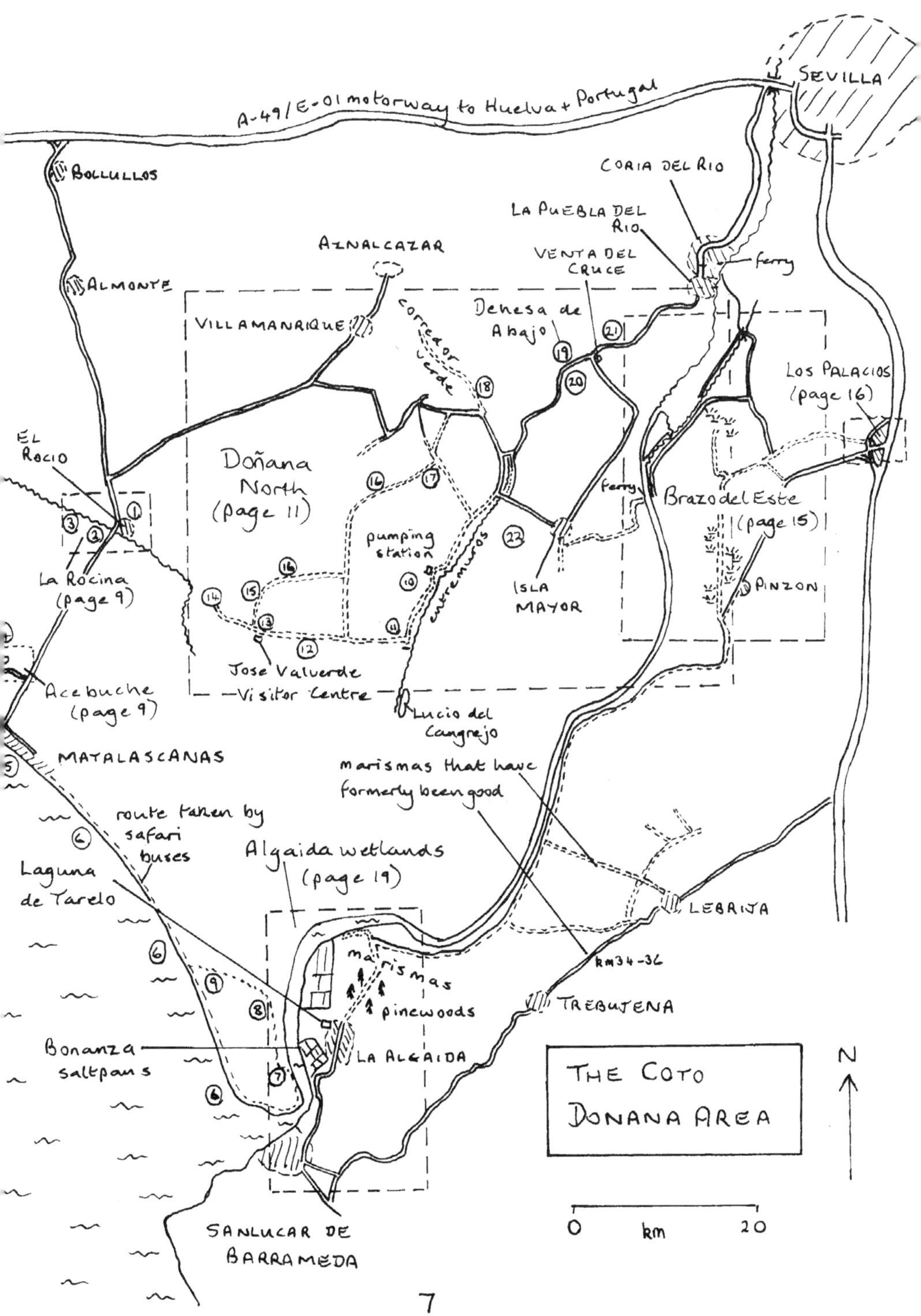

SEVILLA
A-49/E-01 motorway to Huelva + Portugal
BOLLULLOS
CORIA DEL RIO
LA PUEBLA DEL RIO
AZNALCAZAR
VENTA DEL CRUCE
ferry
ALMONTE
Dehesa de Abajo
VILLAMANRIQUE
corredor verde
LOS PALACIOS (page 16)
EL ROCIO
Doñana North (page 11)
ferry
Brazo del Este (page 15)
pumping station
entremuros
La Rocina (page 9)
ISLA MAYOR
PINZON
Jose Valverde Visitor Centre
Acebuche (page 9)
Lucio del Cangrejo
MATALASCANAS
marismas that have formerly been good
route taken by safari buses
Algaida wetlands (page 19)
Laguna de Tarelo
LEBRIJA
marismas
km34-36
pinewoods
TREBUJENA
Bonanza saltpans
LA ALGAIDA
THE COTO DONANA AREA
N
0 km 20
SANLUCAR DE BARRAMEDA

marshy valley of Arroyo de la Rocina (aka. Charco de la Boca). From the hides you should look for species such as Red-crested Pochard, Purple Gallinule, Whiskered Tern, Gull-billed Tern, Marsh Harrier and Glossy Ibis. The nature trail takes you through a good selection of habitats including pine forest, heathland and reedbed. You should therefore find a variety of warblers including Cetti's, Great Reed, Reed, Melodious, Sardinian and, with patience, Dartford Warblers. I've had both Savi's and Grasshopper Warblers here and in spring there are Iberian Chiffchaffs too. The boardwalk path after the second hide is a good spot for Penduline Tits. Listen for Short-toed Treecreepers in the pines and Woodlarks on the heath, and keep an eye open for raptors, especially Booted Eagles; there's a chance of Black-shouldered Kites too.

3. By driving through the car park at La Rocina you follow a road which leads to the Palacio de Acebron. It's worth looking along here for species such as Thekla Lark, Iberian Chiffchaff and Black-shouldered Kite but it is best known as a stake-out for Red-Necked Nightjar. By driving along this road at dusk you should at least hear them and, especially if the day has been hot, you may even see several them sitting on the road itself giving fantastic views.

4. The reception centre at Acebuche (pronounced 'athay-boochay') is next to the Laguna del Acebuche which can be worth a visit. Although there is plenty of open water here, much of it is obscured by reedy islands so, if you only plan a brief visit, you may be disappointed. If you want to get a complete picture of what's about, you'll need to visit several of the 7 hides and wait patiently for birds to appear. I've seen Purple Gallinule, Red-crested Pochard, Marbled Duck and Ferruginous Duck here but, like the Red-knobbed Coot that bred here in 2007, I suspect some of them at least were released here. Others have had Little Crake, Little Bittern and Moustached Warbler. Look out too for raptors over the heathland to the north; as well as Red and Black Kite, Booted Eagle and Short-toed Eagle, I've had superb views of Spanish Imperial Eagle from here and Black-shouldered Kite is now a possibility too. Azure-winged Magpies often home-in on the picnic tables next to the car park, usually giving superb views. Other birds I've had around here include Great Spotted Cuckoo and Dartford Warbler. The nature trail continues west from her to hides overlooking other lagoons but these are often too dry to be of interest.The safari-tours depart from the visitor centre at about 8.00 each morning.

5. Matalascañas is a tourist resort whose very existence threatens to destroy the nearby marismas since the use of so many toilets, showers and swimming pools places a great burden on the water table in the marshes. However, you may still wish to visit here, if only to do some sea-watching from the beach. Cory's Shearwaters, Yellow-legged and Mediterranean Gulls are regularly seen, but look out too for Gull-billed Tern, Slender-billed and Audouin's Gulls and Arctic Skua.

6. Whilst it is possible to walk down the beach from Matalascañas towards the mouth of the Guadalquivir, I would not recommend it. Even in a safari bus, this trip seems to take ages and in February yielded only Lesser Black-backed Gulls, Sanderlings, Oystercatchers etc. plus lots of offshore Common Scoters and two Peregrines. To reach this area (and sites 7-9) you need to take one of the safari bus tours. These have to be booked in advance with the Co-operativa Marismas del Rocio (Tel:+34 (959) 43 04 32).

7. Visitors on either the boat trip from Sanlucar or the safari trip from Acebuche are taken to La Plancha where an idyllic clearing in the forest is usually occupied by lots of Red Deer, Fallow Deer and Wild Boar. Short-toed Treecreepers and Azure-winged Magpies are abundant and this is a good spot for raptors; in February I had Booted Eagle, Buzzard and Red Kite.

8. Another stop is made at a point overlooking the Lucio del Membrillo. This can be a spectacular lagoon, filled with hundreds, if not thousands, of ducks, geese, waders and

9

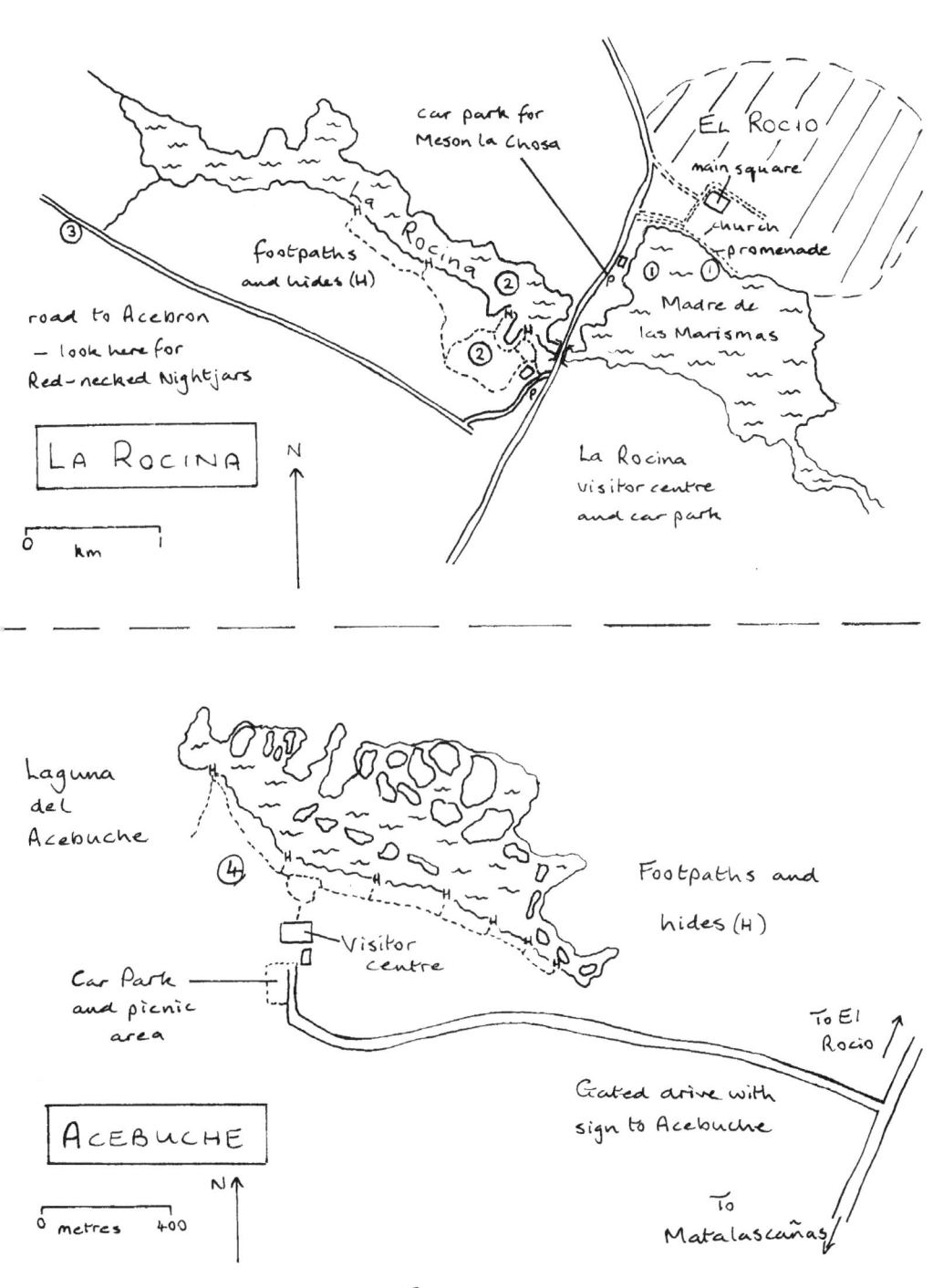

flamingoes. However, in the dry winter of 94/95 I saw only a couple of hundred birds here, just small and distant flocks of Greylags, Wigeon and Black-tailed Godwits. Look in the distance for one or more Spanish Imperial Eagles on the isolated eucalyptus trees in front of the sand-dunes to the north. I did see one but, even with a scope, the views were lousy.

9. A stop amongst the sand-dunes gives you a chance to walk to a high vantage point and scan for raptors. Short-toed Eagles should be easy to see in summer; in February I managed an adult Spanish Imperial Eagle.

To reach the remaining areas from El Rocio you need to head north on the main A-483 road. About 2.5 km out of town, just after km post 13, take the tarmac road to the right, signposted to Villamanrique. After a further 16 km take a right fork (37.21875N 6.34357W), opposite a sign saying "Villamanrique 4km", and continue for about 4km before turning right at the second obvious crossroads (37.21254N 6.29884W). This road leads to a T-junction where you turn left. After a further 2km, turn right just before a Arroyo de la Cigueña where marshy meadows are excellent for egrets, storks and Squacco Herons. You are now at the northern end of a loop that can be followed in either direction to the Centro Visitantes Jose Valverde which is well-signposted. Note however that most of this route is on rough, pot-holed gravel tracks which have to be followed for about 50km (yes, fifty!) to complete the circuit.

10. Park by the large white building here (37.10566N 6.25831W) which is the main pumping station (Casa de Bombas). To the east you should scan for waterbirds, especially in and around the irrigation channel (Entremuros). Apart from typical species such as Purple Heron, this can be a good spot for Kingfisher, Bluethroat, Glossy Ibis, Black Stork and Great Bittern. In winter, the flat open fields to the west will have up to 2000 cranes, 10,000 Greylag Geese and impressive numbers of raptors. These will be mostly Kestrels, Buzzards and Marsh Harriers, but Hen Harriers, Red Kites, Peregrines, Merlins and Black-shouldered Kites are also likely. In spring and summer there are fewer raptors but look out for Short-toed and Booted Eagles and Montagu's Harriers amongst the ubiquitous Black Kites.

11. Similar species can also be looked for from the point where the road turns sharply west (37.07132N 6.27183W). In the distance, due east from here, is a copse with a few eucalyptus trees. Spanish Imperial Eagles have bred there so it's worth scanning that area with a scope.

12. On my visit in December 2008 I found the east-west road to the visitor centre to be the most productive for birds such as Black-shouldered Kite, Little Bustard and Stone Curlew – just keep scanning the fields to the north. This is also a good area for Pin-tailed Sandgrouse, Collared Pratincole and both species of Short-toed Larks of which Lesser Short-toed is by far the least numerous and is likely to be missed unless you know their calls. To the south of this road are shallow wetlands (*Lucios*) which, when flooded, invariably have flamingoes and stilts and in winter will have flocks of coot and ducks. Apparently Red-knobbed Coot have been seen here. Many of the roadside sparrows here will be Spanish Sparrows.

13. The Jose Valverde visitor centre (37.07348N 6.37780W) overlooks an area of pools (the Lucio Cerrado Garrido) to the south and a copse of tamarisks to the west. In spring and summer the tamarisks are occupied by hundreds of nesting egrets and ibis and you get great views of these from inside the centre or, better still, by standing outside at the corner of the building. Purple Heron, Squacco Heron and Night Heron breed here too and there's even been a Western Reef Heron paired with one of the Little Egrets. You can get particularly close to Purple Gallinules here and this is one of the best spots in the Doñana area for seeing difficult species such as Little Bittern and the rarer crakes. The pools to the south can be teeming with waterfowl but only the

Doñana from the North

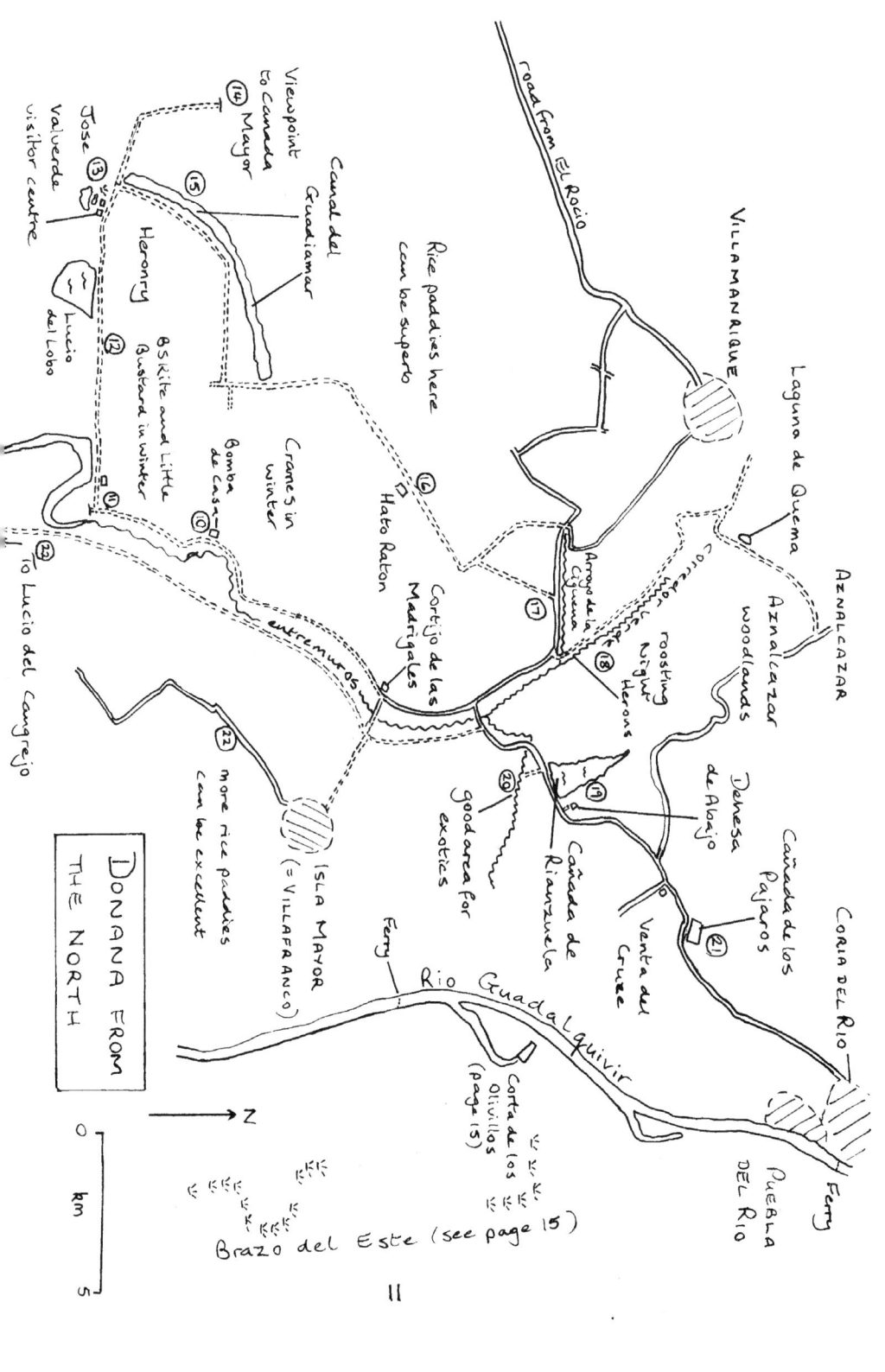

nearest pool can be seen well from the centre and even then the light is usually against you. This is said to be a good area for Marbled Duck and Red-knobbed Coot but maybe they prefer the pools that are tantalizingly just out of view. Oh, for an observation tower.

14. The road from the visitor centre directly to El Rocio is now blocked but is often worth following as far as you can before turning back again. This allows you to overlook more wetland areas but also gets you as close as possible to the Cañada Mayor area. This is excellent for raptors, especially kites and Booted Eagles but also vultures (mostly Griffon, but sometimes Black or Egyptians too) and Spanish Imperial Eagles.

15. The drive north from the visitor centre takes you alongside the Caño del Guadiamar, another wetland that usually holds plenty of water and hence offers more views of species such as Purple Heron, Squacco Heron, Black-necked Grebe, Gull-billed Tern, Collared Pratincole and Purple Gallinule. Little Bittern and White-headed duck have also been seen here.

16. One of the best areas in winter is around the Hato Raton farm building (37.15575N 628362W). The fields here have been turned into rice paddies, some of which can be chock full of birds - just look wherever you see gatherings of storks or herons. Amongst them you should see numbers of duck and a surprising variety of waders plus wagtails and pipits including, in winter, Water Pipits. Bear in mind though that there are some times of year (eg March) when the rice fields are dry and practically birdless.

17. Just before you return to the Arroyo de Cigueñas you drive through an area of grazed fields (37.18791N 6.24938W) which represent one of the best areas for Montagu's Harrier, Pin-tailed Sandgrouse, Collared Pratincole and Little Bustard. I've also had a feeding flock of Lesser Kestrels here.

18. There's a track that leads north from the Arroyo de Cigueñas towards Aznalcazar. This follows a route known as the Corredor Verde (Green Corridor) an area which was poisoned by toxic waste in 1998 but has since been encouraged to regenerate. The lush greenery now supports species such as Western Olivaceous Warbler and Rufous Bush Chat and this is one of the best areas for Black-shouldered Kite (eg 10 in May 2006 – David and Amanda Mason); the bridge where the track crosses the channel (37.24593N 6.26752W) has become a particularly popular spot to look for them. At the beginning of this track (37.20436N 6.22458W), the tamarisks by the canal provide a roosting area for dozens, maybe hundreds, of Night Herons, though most of them remain hidden during the day. At the far end, via a ford which isn't always passable, is a reservoir, the Laguna de Quema (37.25420N 6.26000W) which is particularly good for diving ducks including Tufted Duck – a species you're likely to miss elsewhere. Beyond the reservoir are the pinewoods of Aznalcazar where I've had Long-eared and Eagle Owl as well as Red-necked Nightjar, Azure-winged Magpie, Crested Tit and Woodlark.

19. By taking the road towards Venta del Cruce you'll reach one of Doñana's most important wetlands – a sizeable lake called the Cañada de Rianzuela. This can be viewed either from the road or via the paths which lead down from the visitor centre at the Dehesa de Abajo (37.20594N 6.17100W). In winter the lake has large numbers of duck and coot and represents the best opportunity in the Doñana area to see both White-headed Duck and Red-knobbed Coot. The rarer coots are typically found close to the edges rather than out amongst the rafts of other coot in the middle of the lake. I had at least half-a-dozen in December 2008 by the eastern shore and a pair in March 2009 in the south-east corner. Some of them can be easily picked out because they are wearing conspicuous dog-collars, indicating that they have been released from a captive breeding program just up the road at Cañada de los Pajaros but there are now plenty that are unadorned. The White-headed Ducks should be easily found, at least in

winter, by scanning with a scope through the flocks of duck which usually include Red-crested Pochard and, occasionally, Marbled Duck too. In spring you should see Black-necked Grebes and Great Reed Warblers from the road. During passage times, if the water levels are low, the lake can be excellent for herons (including up to a dozen Great White Egret), waders (eg huge flocks of stilts and Avocets) and marsh terns (all three species have been seen). The Dehesa de Abajo is famous for having the largest tree-nesting colony of White Storks in Spain but those same trees also hold large numbers of nesting raptors, mostly Black Kite but also Red Kite and Booted Eagle. Spanish Imperial Eagles have also been seen by scanning north from the visitor centre. Close to the centre you should find a pair of Southern Grey Shrikes – listen for their 'glip-glip' calls – and, in summer, lots of Bee-eaters which nest in the sandy banks nearby.

20. By taking a track (37.19699N 6.18412W) which leads south from the road at the south-west corner of the Cañada de Rianzuela you can drive to one of the main water channels in the area – the Brazo de la Torre. This quiet, undisturbed site is one of the best places to look for reed-bed species such as Penduline Tit, Little Bittern, Purple Heron and Savi's Warbler. Birders might particularly want to visit here to look for two new exotic species that have become established Black-rumped Waxbill and Yellow-crowned Bishop. The best plan is to walk along the edges of the channel, checking the reeds and other areas of weedy vegetation.

21. Just east of the Venta del Cruce is a 'bird park', Cañada de los Pajaros, (37.23831N 6.12918W) which is basically a zoo which specializes in the native species of that area. I haven't visited here myself but I'm told it can be a great place for photographers to get natural-looking shots of species such as herons and waterfowl.

22. By turning east from the Cortijo de las Madrigales you can cross the Entremuros channel and explore the Isla Mayor area. This is another area where the old marismas have been turned into rice paddies but, if water levels are right, these can still be fantastic for birds. The tracks on this side of the Entremuros take you further south and closer to the Lucio del Cangrejo, should you wish to explore that area.

Brazo del Este
(including Pinzon Marshes)

Attraction

An area of pools, channels and reedbeds which can be quite outstanding for waterbirds, especially Purple Gallinules. The marshes near Pinzon were the subject of a mouth-watering article in Birding World, but for a while they were dry and completely useless for birds! However, a succession of wet years has restored them to their former glory. They are just one of several wetland areas on the east bank of the Guadalquivir that deserve more attention from birders.

Getting there

All parts of the Brazo del Este can be reached via Los Palacios y Villafranca. There is a new 'ring road' (N-IV) around the west of town and from this you can turn right into Los Palacios (by the football stadium) or left towards Pinzon and the southern end of these marshes. The northern end can be reached by taking the ferry from Coria del Rio, crossing the bridge and continuing until you reach the warehouse of Mediterraneo Algadon (37.20719N 6.02237W). The other ferry, between here and Isla Mayor, isn't always operational. I've gone to some trouble to ensure you can then navigate to and between all the best areas by following the tracks and bridges shown on this map.

Notes

1. Chris Hancock's description of the Pinzon Marshes (Birding World Vol 6: page 243) tells of how, in 1993, he found lots of Purple Gallinule (37 at once), Purple Heron, Spoonbills, Great Reed Warbler, Fan-tailed Warbler, Grasshopper Warbler, Black Tern, Whiskered Tern, Night Heron, Red-crested Pochard, Marsh Harrier and Gull-billed Tern plus smaller numbers of Black Stork, Glossy Ibis, Short-toed Eagle, Osprey, Little Crake, Spotted Crake, and Collared Pratincole. In February and April 1995 the marshes were completely dry but in March 2009 there was plenty of water and I found many of the same species listed above, (though not the crakes, storks, osprey or pratincoles) as well as Great White Egret. Both Marbled Duck and Red-knobbed Coot are said to have bred here in recent years and this is one of the best sites for the escaped exotics including Yellow-crowned Bishop. To get here, drive 3 km beyond Pinzon to the T-junction next to some tall silos (37.08150N 6.03889W). Take the track to the right and follow this for 2 km until marshes, or at least their remnants, come into view. To explore the most extensive wetland, take the track to the east (37.10820N 6.03771W) around the large, reed-infested oxbow lake. Another good spot is the large reed-fringed pool (La Margazuela) to the west of the track (37.1288N 6.03729W). If these marshes are dry, continue further North.

2. The long channel through the middle of the reserve has reeds along much of its length and therefore looks promising for warblers and crakes. I had several Penduline Tits here in February, plus a Barn Owl roosting in a willow. Bluethroats also occur in winter.

3. This most northerly area of marsh, apparently known as Conde Chico, was rather disappointing on my last visit in March 2009. However, in a dry year this can be one of the few wetlands that persist. In such circumstances, in February and April 1995 I saw lots of egrets, waders and warblers including Squacco Heron, Collared Pratincole and Savi's Warbler plus Black Stork, Water Pipit, Gull-billed Tern, 'flocks' of Purple Gallinules and a Little Crake. The easiest way to get there is to turn west at the Mediterraneo Algadon warehouse and the marshes will appear on your left after about 2 km. You can walk to the edge of the marsh via the next track to the left, 1.2 km further on (37.20006N 6.06241W).

BRAZO DEL ESTE

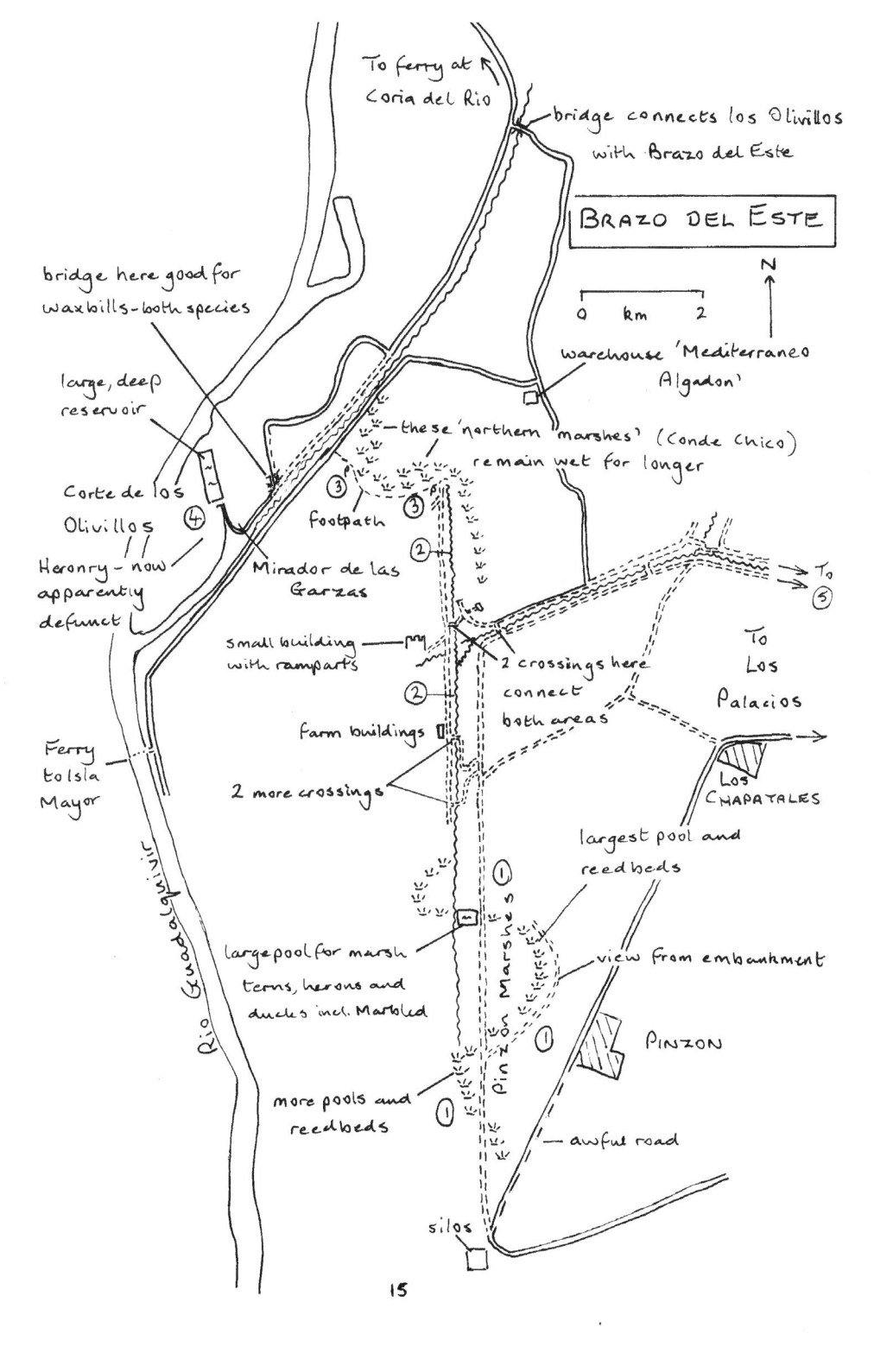

To ferry at Coria del Rio

bridge connects los Olivillos with Brazo del Este

N ↑

0 km 2

warehouse 'Mediterraneo Algodon'

bridge here good for waxbills - both species

large, deep reservoir

these 'northern marshes' (Conde Chico) remain wet for longer

Corte de los Olivillos ④

Heronry - now apparently defunct

③ ③ footpath

②

Mirador de las Garzas

small building with ramparts

2 crossings here connect both areas

To ⑤

To Los Palacios

②

farm buildings

2 more crossings

Ferry to Isla Mayor

Los Chapatales

largest pool and reedbeds

①

view from embankment

large pool for marsh terns, herons and ducks incl. Marbled

Rio Guadalquivir

Pinzon Marshes

①

PINZON

more pools and reedbeds

①

awful road

silos

15

4. The Corta de los Olivillos looks like it should be a fantastic spot. There's a good-sized deep-water pool and, supposedly, a heronry in a little visited 'island' at the confluence of two major branches of the river. However, in March 2009 it was very disappointing. The main pool had very few birds, mostly Cormorants and a few duck and from the nearby Mirador de las Garzas (Viewpoint of the Egrets – 37.18777N 6.08157W) I saw less than a dozen herons despite staying until dusk hoping for a 'spectacular roost'. The colony (described only recently as 'one of the biggest in Spain') seems to be deserted. At least 4 Marsh Harriers roosted here. Nearby, where there's a little bridge over a channel (37.19391N 6.07423W) I had small parties of waxbills including both Common Waxbill and Black-rumped Waxbill. Red Avadavat is said to be in this area too. To reach this area, turn south at the bridge over the Nuevo Guadaira (37.24651N 6.02484W) keeping on the west bank of that river.

5. A small wetland called Laguna de la Mejorada or Laguna de Diego Puertas (but widely known as Los Palacios lagoon) has become popular amongst birders as a reliable site for Western Olivaceous Warbler. To get there, take the 'old' Seville road north from Los Palacios and, 2.3km after leaving the town, turn right along a track immediately before a bridge over a water channel (37.19067N 5.92438W). By keeping right you can follow this track around the lagoon and park at the north-west corner. Up to 6 Olivaceous Warblers have been heard singing in the tamarisks; other species to look for here include Rufous Bush Chat, Penduline Tit and Common Waxbill. The lake itself has Black-necked Grebes and Purple Gallinules and is a great place for breeding and roosting herons: in addition to the spectacular roost of Cattle Egrets, you could find Night Heron, Squacco Heron and Purple Heron.

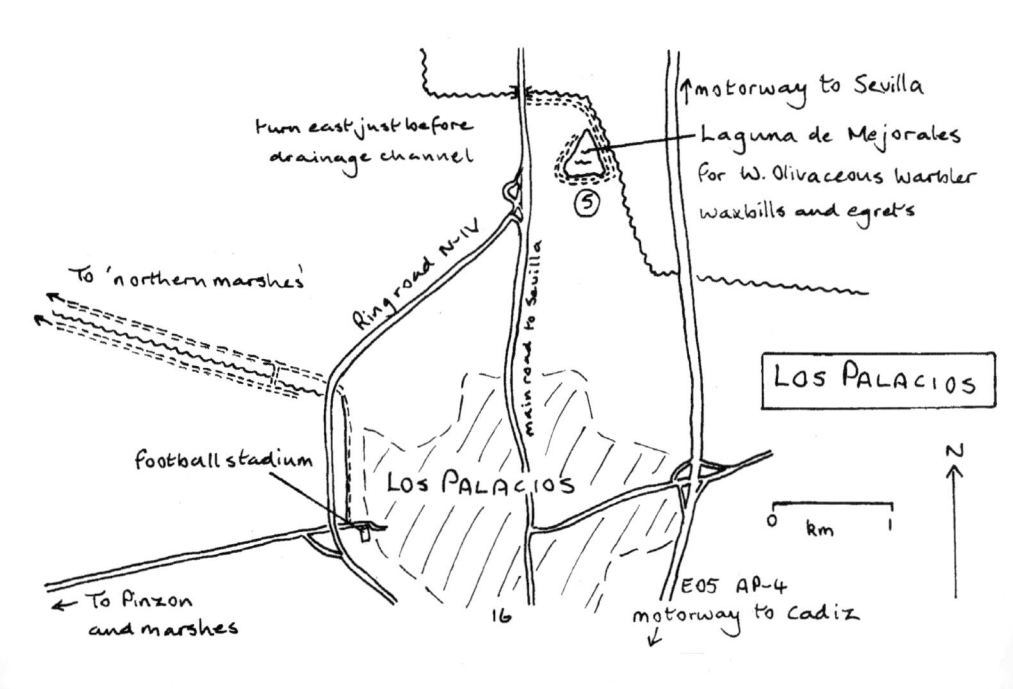

La Algaida area

(including Laguna de Tarelo, Bonanza Salinas, Monte Algaida Salinas and Trebujena marismas)

Attraction

The eastern bank of the Guadalquivir has two extensive areas of saltpans which are always good for waterbirds, especially waders, gulls, terns and flamingoes. In addition, a new sand-pit has been created, the Laguna de Tarelo which has been a real hotspot for White-headed Ducks – up to 200 present in winter – and now holds a significant heronry. These sites never dry out and are therefore invaluable refuges when most of the marismas of the Coto Doñana are dry. This eastern side also has a few marismas of its own, where birds such as pratincoles, sandgrouse, Lesser Short-toed Larks and Gull-billed Terns may be found. If these marismas are flooded, they can be teeming with birds including regular Marbled Duck

Getting There

As you enter Sanlucar de Barrameda, look for signs pointing to the right towards Puerto de Bonanza and/or Algaida. Follow this road to a T-junction where you turn left then quickly right onto the road which heads out of the village alongside the river. All the sites can be reached via this road.

Access

Thankfully, it is no longer necessary to get a permit to visit the Bonanza Salinas; these sites are all viewable from public tracks.

Notes

1. Organised boat-trips to the Doñana National Park (site 7, page 5) set off from Bajo de Guia, a beach location between Sanlucar and Bonanza. There's an information centre at Bajo de Guia with very helpful staff. Walk south from the main car park and the centre is on your left.

2. The Bonanza salinas can be excellent for birds, especially towards their northern end. If the water levels are high, the main species will be flamingoes, stilts, avocets and gulls – this is the best place around Doñana to see Slender-billed Gulls. However, lower water levels allow the pans to host hundreds more waders, especially Black-tailed Godwits, 'shanks, Curlew Sandpipers and both species of stint. Look out for Caspian and Gull-billed Terns and Mediterranean and Audouin's Gulls sitting on the embankments between the pans and groups of Black and Whiskered Terns over the water. Flocks of Glossy Ibis sometimes wander in from the Doñana reserve and Red-necked Phalarope is regularly seen here too. From the entrance to the saltpans (36.81766N 6.33496W) you can drive north to a T-junction of tracks which can then be followed in either direction eg right to the white hut where you overlook a tidal pool that can be good for Slender-billed Gull and Glossy Ibis.

3. The Laguna de Tarelo is essentially a sand-pit on the edge of the Coto Doñana. This has been the best place in southern Spain for White-headed Duck; 220 were counted here in December 1994 and over 20 pairs remained during the following summer when some were seen with chicks. More recently, though, there have been fewer in winter and I had none here in April 2009. Dozens more ducks and grebes occur including Black-necked Grebe, Red-crested Pochard and Purple Gallinule and I had Ferruginous Duck too in April 09. An island in the lake is now occupied in spring by dozens of breeding herons, including Spoonbills and Night Herons. Squacco Heron and Little Bittern also

occur around the margins. The pool is found by driving north through Algaida village and turning left along 'Calle Algaida N' (36.84460N 6.31578W). Follow this track until the lake appears on your right, providing excellent views. Alternatively, at the southern entrance to Algaida woods, look for a track to the left (36.84709N 6.31490W) which leads to an observation screen.

4. The road through Algaida continues into an area of pine forest where it badly deteriorates. Despite the picnic parties, these woods still hold species such as Iberian Chiff-chaff, Bonelli's Warbler, Azure-winged Magpie and, at dusk, Red-necked Nightjar. Black Kites are particularly numerous here. The Magpies can be elusive but the picnic sites may attract rather than deter them.

5. At the far end of the wood, turn left and follow the road for about 2 km until it turns sharply right over a bridge. Instead of crossing the canal, take the track (36.90085N 6.29586W) which goes straight ahead and follow this to the left, signposted 'observatorio...' along the top of the first embankment. This drive allows you to overlook an area of marismas where, Lesser Short-toed and Calandra Larks are likely and, if conditions are wet, waders and egrets can be numerous. You may have to park after about 2km; beyond here the embankment, which skirts the Monte Algaida saltpans, is precariously narrow in places and even the better track which follows the foot of the embankment can be impassable to most vehicles. For the next 4km you should regularly mount the embankment to scan over the saltpans and look through the hundreds of waterbirds (flamingoes, cormorants, spoonbills etc). Eventually you reach the 'observatorio' (36.87596N 6.34350W) - a screen which allows you to observe the birds without them seeing you. From here you can continue to walk south, through saltmarsh which is particularly good for Lesser Short-toed Lark (I've had up to 10 here) to a point overlooking a huge lagoon. In winter this can be teeming with birds including thousands of ducks, waders and flamingoes. Unfortunately these can only be seen from a distance and, for most of the day, against the light; however, in some seasons this lagoon can be dry and birdless.

6. The road which goes east from the aforementioned bridge passes an area of marismas (sometimes described as Trebujena Marismas) where, especially between the road and the river, you may find some promising pools and marshes (36.89605N 6.2800W). This is one of the best sites around Doñana for Marbled Duck; White-headed Duck, and even Red-knobbed Coot, are sometimes found here too. Depending on the water levels this area could be excellent for waders and terns (including Gull-billed and Caspian) and the drier areas should be scanned in winter for Pin-tailed Sandgrouse and Stone Curlew.

7. The area around Trebujena has largely been converted from marismas to agricultural land. I can't confirm whether the areas I previously described (about 5km west of Lebrija and between km 34 and km 36 on the A-471 between Trebujena and Lebrija) still support the classic marismas species (Pin-tailed Sandgrouse, Stone Curlew, Lesser-short-toed Lark, Spectacled Warbler and Montagu's Harrier) or whether Lesser Kestrels and Little Bustards can still be found there but I notice that Moreno and Gutierrez (2006) recommend a different site where they say the classic species still occur. To get there, take the road between Sanlucar and Trebujena and turn north on a track by km post 51.8 (36.79478N 6.26023W). You can follow this track for 3.1 kilometres before crossing a bridge and returning via another track down the other side of the dyke, scanning all the time for birds.

Algaida Wetlands

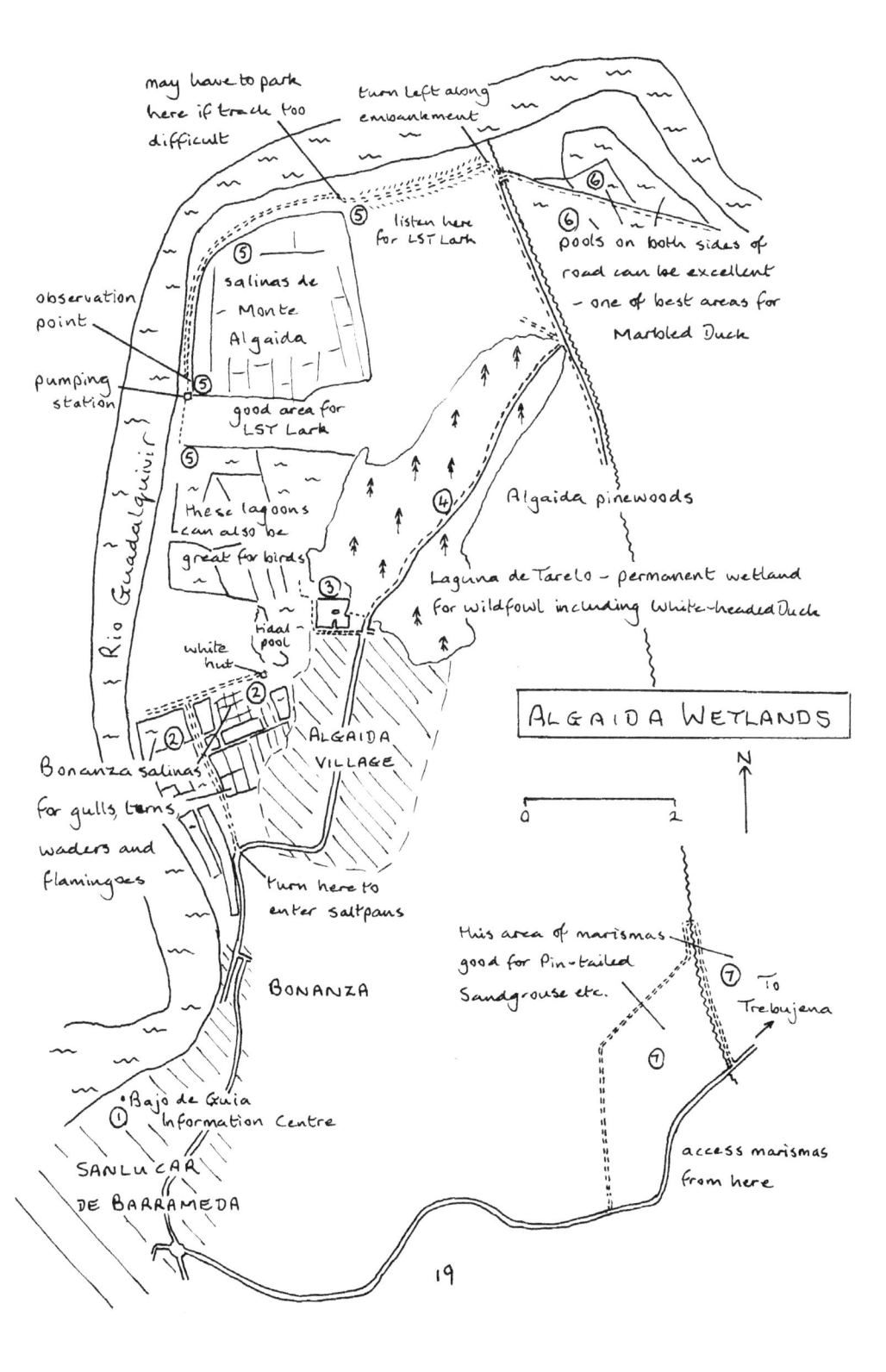

may have to park here if track too difficult

turn left along embankment

⑤ *listen here for LST Lark*

⑥ *pools on both sides of road can be excellent — one of best areas for Marbled Duck*

observation point

pumping station

⑤ Salinas de Monte Algaida

⑤ *good area for LST Lark*

⑤ *These lagoons can also be great for birds*

④ Algaida pinewoods

Rio Guadalquivir

③ tidal pool

white hut

② ② Algaida Village

Laguna de Tarelo — permanent wetland for wildfowl including White-headed Duck

ALGAIDA WETLANDS

N ↑

0 — 2

Bonanza salinas for gulls, terns, waders and flamingoes

turn here to enter saltpans

BONANZA

This area of marismas good for Pin-tailed Sandgrouse etc.

⑦ To Trebujena

⑦

access marismas from here

① Bajo de Guia Information Centre

SANLUCAR DE BARRAMEDA

19

The Jerez Lagoons

(Laguna de Medina, the Lagunas de Terry and the Lagunas de Puerto Real)

Attraction

In the area around Jerez are a number of lakes which can be quite excellent for waterbirds, including such specialities as White-headed Duck, Red-knobbed Coot and Marbled Duck. In dry years, if you can't find these birds around the Coto Doñana, these other sites may be worth trying. The Laguna de Medina should be the first place to visit but, if this is dry too, then sites like Laguna de Taraje become vital. All these sites, if wet, are also good for birds like Black-necked Grebe, Purple Gallinule and Red-crested Pochard. For some time, the location of these lagoons has been supposedly secret but they are now widely publicised and often signposted.

Getting There

The lagoons described here can all be reached from the A-381 between Jerez and Medina Sidonia, although the Lagunas de Santa Maria are easier to get to from the CA-31 just north of El Puerto de Santa Maria.

Access

Of the lagoons mentioned here, only sites 3 and 4 are private, the rest can be easily viewed, without any fear of disturbance, from public roads and tracks.

Notes

1. The most famous and, potentially, the best of these lakes, the Laguna de Medina, is easily visible just to the east of the A-381, 10 km south of Jerez and 30 km north of Medina. At the junction with the A-3202 (approx 36.618N 6.066W) there's a road to the east signposted to 'Laguna de Medina' which leads to the car park 36.61353N 6.05840W. There's a path around the whole lake but the stretch along the south side is best. When the lake has plenty of water, there will be lots of waterbirds, especially flamingoes, coots ducks and grebes but these can be hard to view because many bushes have grown up between the path and the lake. Thankfully there is now an excellent hide, about 900 metres from the car park. The views from here are great although you do have to look through glazed windows. In early April 2009, White-headed Duck, Black-necked Grebe, Red-crested Pochard and Purple Gallinule were all easily visible close to the hide and I heard Red-knobbed Coot and Little Bittern too. Montero (2005) reports that almost 800 White-headed Duck have been counted in winter and up to 10 pairs of Red-knobbed Coot have bred – they are more likely to be found around the reedy margins than out in the open water with the other rafts of Coot. Marbled Duck is also possible here; I've had up to 10 here myself. In dry years the water may dry up altogether or shrink to a pool in the middle. Its muddy margins can then be great for waders such as Avocet, Ruff, Black-tailed Godwit and Collared Pratincole. Contrary to what it seems to say on the sign in the car park, the walk around the lake is over 4km and would take a lot longer than 30 minutes. However, just by going to the hide and back you should find birds such as Great Reed, Cetti's, Fan-tailed, Sardinian, Subalpine and Melodious Warblers (by the car park) plus Nightingale and Woodchat Shrike. Look out for Penduline Tit in winter.

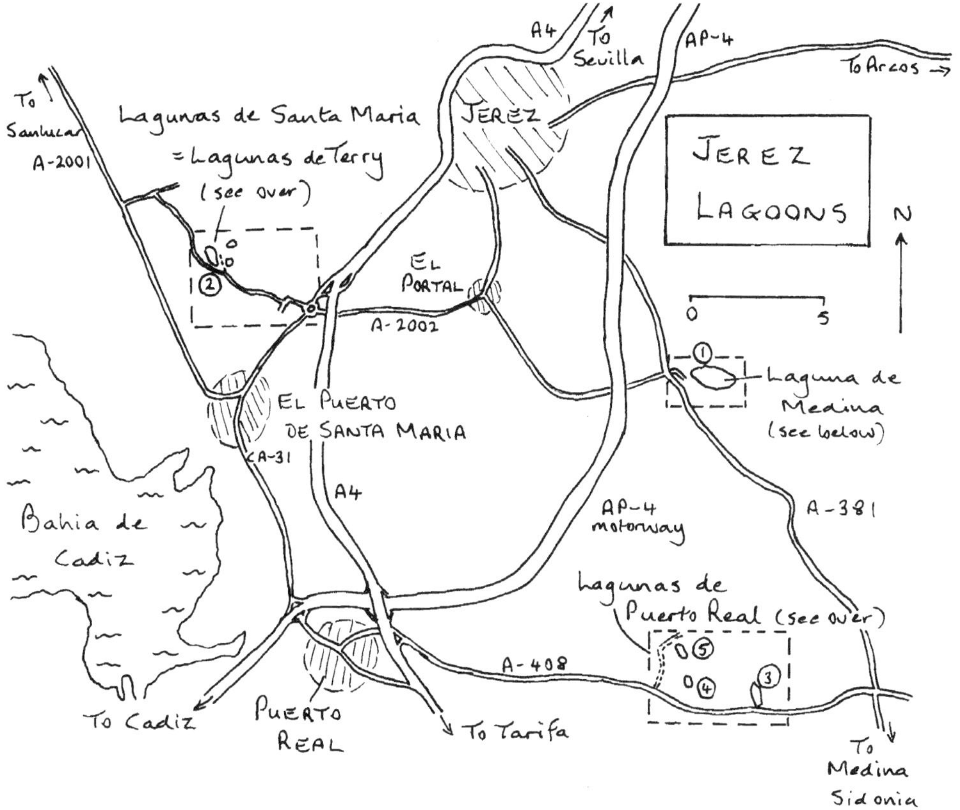

LAGUNA DE MEDINA

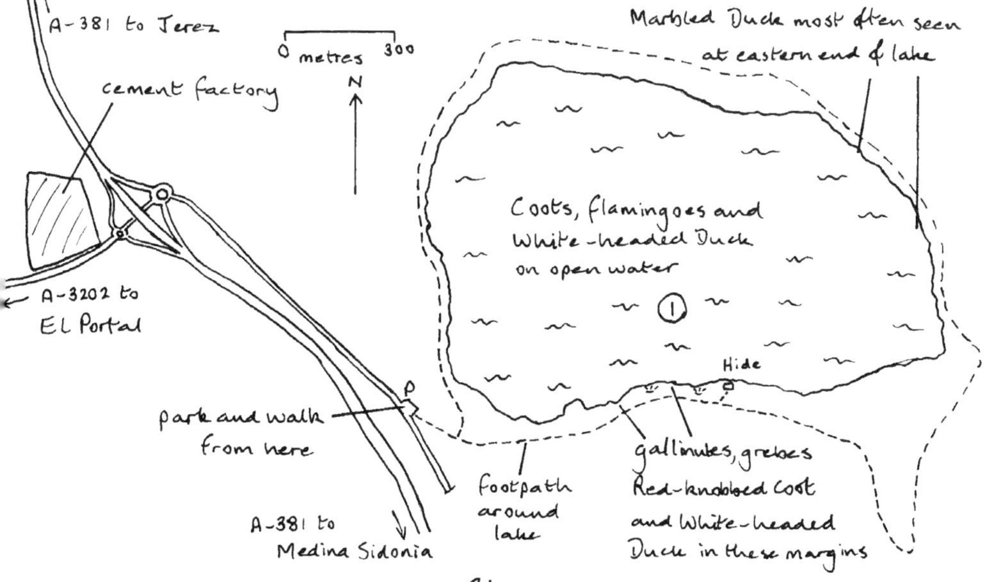

2. The Laguna Salada is the biggest and best of a group of lakes, sometimes known collectively as the Lagunas de Puerto de Santa Maria or Lagunas de Terry. In April 2009 Laguna Salada had plenty of water but only a limited selection of birds, the best of which were Black-necked Grebe, Red-crested Pochard and a Pintail. The Laguna Juncosa had virtually no visible water but I still had Marsh Harrier, Purple Gallinule, Red-crested Pochard and Collared Pratincole here. To get to these lakes, turn west off the CA-31 at the roundabout by the Aquasherry Park, then turn right immediately after a left-hand bend around a casino. After 1km pull onto the track to the right (36.63639N 6.22726W), next to Laguna Juncosa. Walk this track for 900 metres then turn left past the lone white hut (36.64350N 6.23250W) to reach the shore of Laguna Salada. There doesn't seem to be a path around the lake but you can overlook it from various spots shown on the map. Laguna Chica is down the track to the right but this was marked by a 'no entry' sign in 2009.

3. The Laguna de Comisario is private but some of it can just be seen without crossing any fences. From the Laguna de Medina, drive south on the A-381 for 13.5 km then turn right (west) along the A-408. After nearly 4km, look for a track to the right on the (rather dangerous) brow of a hill, immediately before a stand of eucalyptus trees (36.51851N 6.02357W). This track leads to the lake but a gate prevents you from getting beyond the eucalyptus plantation. By scanning from near the gate you can see only a fraction of the lake and you may attract the attention of a 'guardian'. This can be to your advantage if you can persuade him to let you walk beyond the gate. In this way I've managed to see Purple Gallinule, Red-crested Pochard and Black-necked Grebe here (and others have had Marbled Duck too) but from the gate you'd be lucky to see more than a Marsh Harrier. In some years the lake will be dry anyway.

4. In 2009 I tried to reach the Laguna de San Antonio from the Laguna de Taraje but failed to find the right track (see site 5). Back in 1995, I did accidentally locate this lake but I was soon confronted by a 'guardian' who pointed out that the track I'd taken, past 'La Micona' farmhouse, was actually private. For the record then, I would say that it's not worth getting into trouble for, even though it had plenty of water in such a dry winter. Mallard, Little Grebe, Marsh Harrier, Grey Heron and Black-headed Gulls were the only waterbirds I saw but there was masses of emergent vegetation in which Purple Gallinules were surely lurking. It is reputedly good for Little Bittern too.

5. The Laguna de Taraje is a beautiful lake tucked away in a quiet area of countryside. It is one of the last Andalucian lagoons to dry up. Normally you should expect birds such as Purple Gallinule, Marsh Harrier, Black-necked Grebe and Red-crested Pochard plus hundreds of other duck and smaller numbers of waders, gulls and terns. However, the rarer species (Marbled Duck, Red-knobbed Coot and White-headed Duck) are also possible here but are more likely to be found at the Laguna de Medina. Taraje is also good for raptors including regular Osprey, Spanish Imperial Eagle and, recently, Black-shouldered Kite. To get there, drive a further 5km west along the A-408 from the Laguna de Comissario and look for a track to the north (36.52565N 6.08388W), through a pine plantation, just after the 'old' km 9 signpost (newer signposts have been built in slightly different locations (!) but if you see a sign to La Carrascosa you know you have the right track). Keep right after 1.4km and drive until the lagoon appears on the right. A little further on is a footpath around the eastern side of the lagoon where Stone Curlews are usually obvious. I expected this path would also lead to Site 4 but realize now that I should have turned left at 36.53242N 6.05590W.

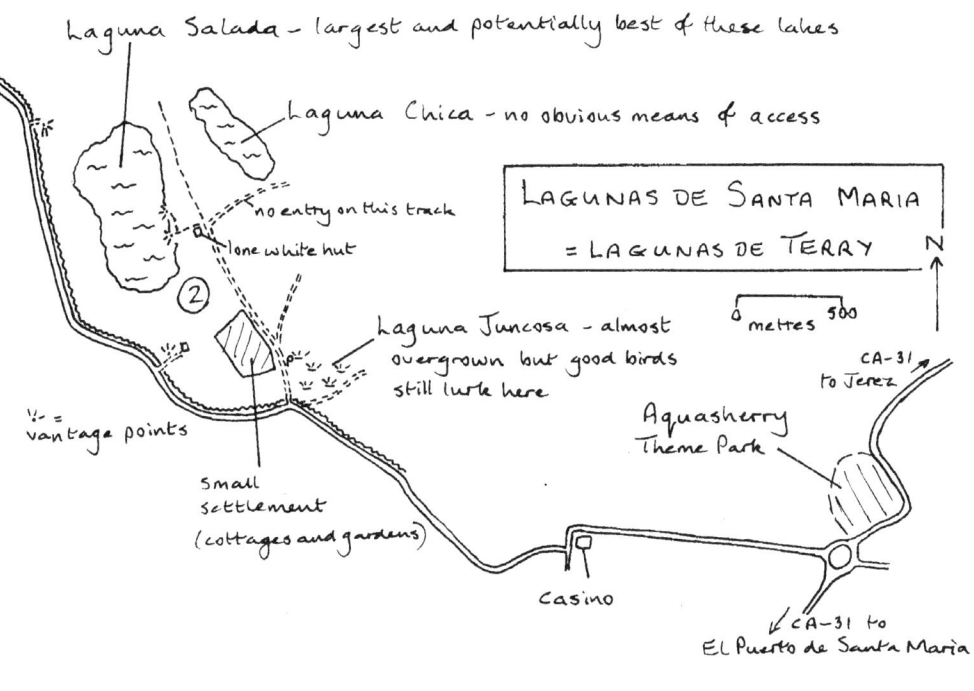

Lagunas de Santa Maria = Lagunas de Terry

- Laguna Salada – largest and potentially best of these lakes
- Laguna Chica – no obvious means of access
- no entry on this track
- lone white hut
- ②
- ⚡ = vantage points
- Laguna Juncosa – almost overgrown but good birds still lurk here
- Small settlement (cottages and gardens)
- Casino
- Aquasherry Theme Park
- CA-31 to Jerez
- CA-31 to El Puerto de Santa Maria
- 0 — 500 metres

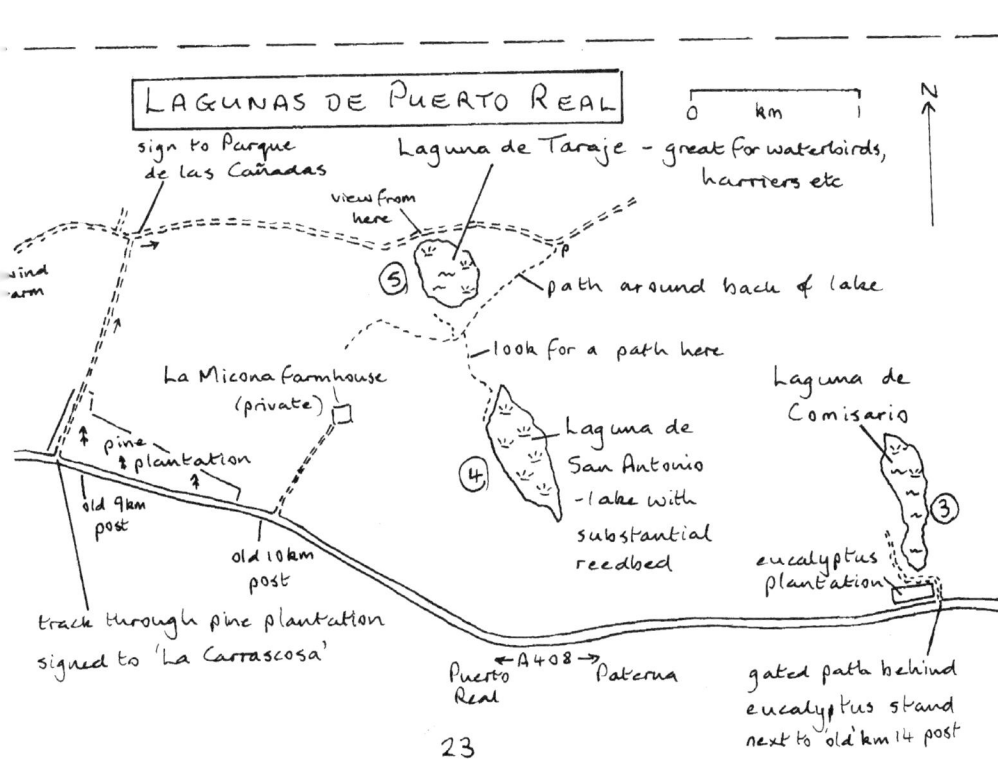

Lagunas de Puerto Real

- sign to Parque de las Cañadas
- Laguna de Taraje – great for waterbirds, harriers etc
- view from here
- ⑤
- path around back of lake
- look for a path here
- La Micona Farmhouse (private)
- pine plantation
- old 9 km post
- old 10 km post
- track through pine plantation signed to 'La Carrascosa'
- ④ Laguna de San Antonio – lake with substantial reedbed
- Laguna de Comisario
- ③
- eucalyptus plantation
- ← A408 → Puerto Real / Paterna
- gated path behind eucalyptus stand next to 'old' km 14 post
- 0 — 1 km

Around Facinas
(The Sierra de la Plata, the Ojen Valley and La Janda plains)

Attraction

In addition to the typical 'countryside birds' of southern Andalucia, this area has some notable specialities: both Little Swift and White-rumped Swift in the Sierra de la Plata, wintering cranes and raptors (including Black-shouldered Kite) at La Janda and woodland birds including Iberian Chiffchaff in the Ojen Valley. Other notable species include Little Bustard, Purple Gallinule and Bonelli's Eagle.

Getting there

Facinas is a small village, just east of the main N-340 (E5) about 18km north-west of Tarifa. All roads leading from there are good for birds.

Notes

1. The Laguna de la Janda used to be a superb wetland with breeding cranes, Purple Herons etc but it was drained during the 1960's. The resultant agricultural plains are still good for certain birds, especially Cattle Egret, Montagu's Harrier, Calandra Lark, Stone Curlew and Collared Pratincole but Andalucia's last breeding Great Bustards have now disappeared and the Little Bustards have become so scarce they can be hard to locate. This decline is probably due to the fact that many of the flower-rich meadows have been replaced by rice paddies. This isn't entirely bad because these paddies can become excellent shallow lagoons at certain times of year, attracting hundreds of storks, egrets, Glossy Ibis, waders and terns plus up to 1000 cranes in winter. Winter is the best time for raptors too: up to 30 Black-shouldered Kites have been counted, both Bonelli's and Spanish Imperial Eagle are regularly seen and there's a chance of Long-legged Buzzard (amongst the Common Buzzards and Hen Harriers) and Ruppell's Vulture (amongst the many Griffons and fewer Blacks). The easiest way to view the area is by turning east from the N-340 at Venta de Retin. The track (36.21101N 5.78979W) is directly opposite the turning to Zahara. Follow this to a T-junction and turn left along an embankment beside a drainage canal. This canal has now been re-colonised by Purple Gallinules and you may see non-breeding herons too, including Purple, Squacco and Night herons. You can follow this track for 10 km until it re-joins the N-340, checking the many poles and wires for raptors and the fields and rice paddies for cranes and waterbirds. Alternatively you can take a track to the right after 5.6km (36.24712N 5.83533W); this gives views over more rice paddies and more areas for raptors until, about 7km further on, you reach a T-junction where there's a promising pool (36.29513N 5.79422W). By turning right here you can drive the 18km back to Facinas past areas that can be terrific for waterbirds if the water levels are suitable.

2. The Sierra de la Plata is famous for being the first place in the Western Palearctic where White-rumped Swifts were found breeding and it is still the best-known site. They can be seen from Atlanterra or Bolonia but it is the Bolonia side that has become more popular, largely because one of the breeding caves is easily visible and also because the same cave has also attracted Europe's first breeding Little Swifts too! Hence it is possible to visit here, especially in late summer and see small numbers of both swifts together. However, they can also be notoriously elusive. I saw none of either species in early May 2009, despite the fact that several Little Swifts at least were seen here in early April and early June. There's a chance of seeing Little Swifts at any time of year but White-rumped Swift is a summer migrant; they've been seen from early May to mid September at least. To get there, follow signs from the N-340 to Bolonia. On arriving at the blissfully uncommercialised coastal village of Bolonia, keep right and continue on that road, past the roman ruins on your left, for almost 5km until you pass under a

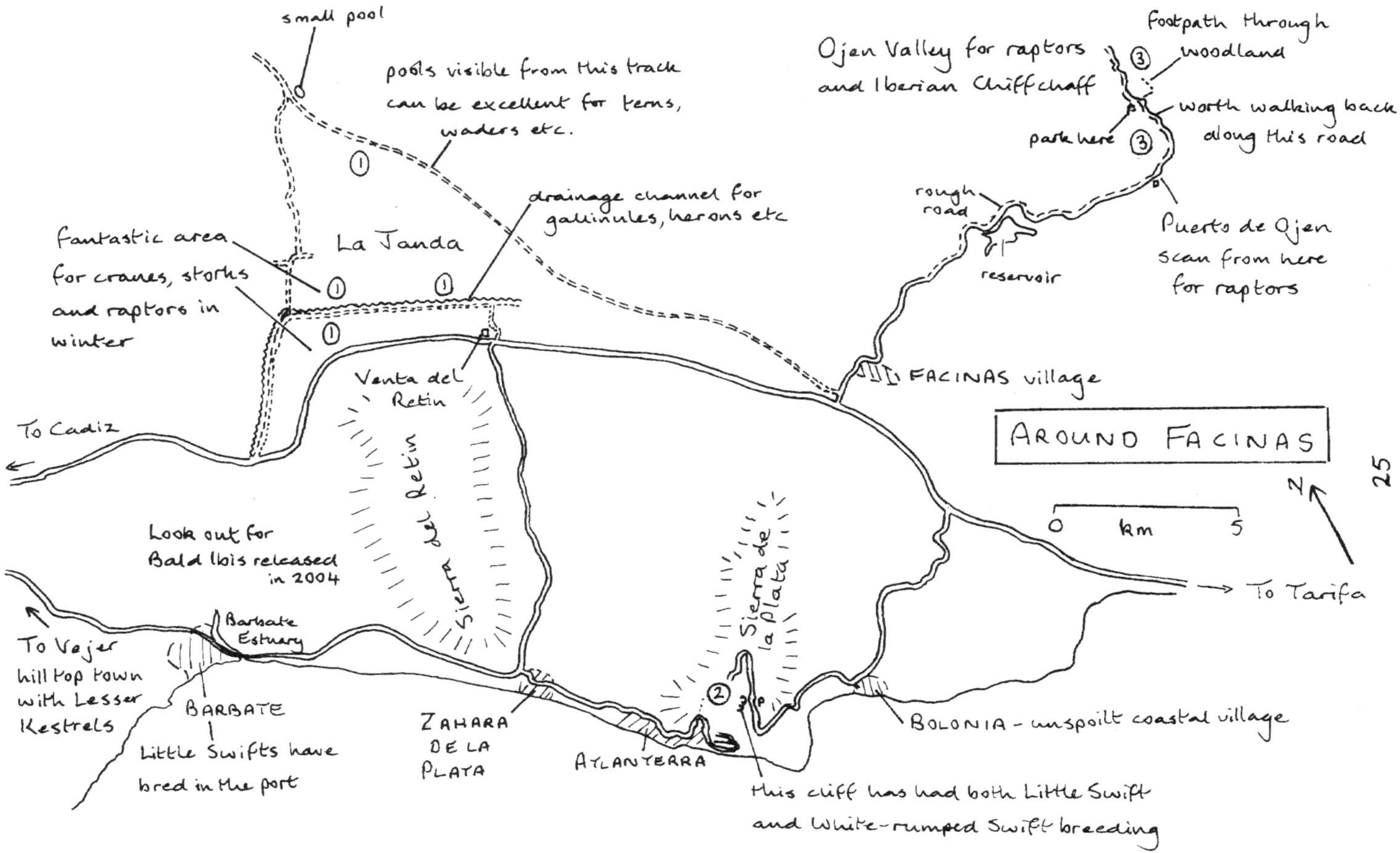
AROUND FACINAS
small pool
pools visible from this track can be excellent for terns, waders etc.
Ojen Valley for raptors and Iberian Chiffchaff
Footpath through woodland
worth walking back along this road
park here
3
3
rough road
reservoir
Puerto de Ojen scan from here for raptors
drainage channel for gallinules, herons etc
La Janda
1
1
1
1
fantastic area for cranes, storks and raptors in winter
Venta del Retin
To Cadiz
FACINAS village
Sierra del Retin
Look out for Bald Ibis released in 2004
Sierra de la Plata
0
km
5
N
To Tarifa
Barbate Estuary
To Vejer hilltop town with Lesser Kestrels
BARBATE
Little Swifts have bred in the port
ZAHARA DE LA PLATA
ATLANTERRA
2
P
BOLONIA - unspoilt coastal village
this cliff has had both Little Swift and White-rumped Swift breeding

steep limestone crag. Park at the lay-by here (36.10025N 5.79312W) and scan around. The cave is obvious, opposite the lay-by; it has a metal grid across, perhaps to protect the swifts. This site also offers exceptional views of Griffon Vultures, which nest on the crag, and other breeding species in the area include Blue Rock Thrush, Egyptian Vulture, Crag Martin, Rock Bunting and Tawny Pipit. The swifts can also be seen in the (same) skies above the Atlanterra side where the scrubby habitat is good for Thekla Lark, Black-eared Wheatear, Subalpine and Dartford Warblers, Red-rumped Swallow and Rock Bunting.

3. The Ojen Valley, East of Facinas, is excellent for birds of prey. Up to 20 Griffon Vulture will be almost constantly in view and you can also expect Egyptian Vulture, Short-toed Eagle, Booted Eagle, Peregrine, Black Kite, Buzzard and Honey Buzzard. Species such as Bonelli's Eagle and Black Vulture are also seen occasionally. The open area around Venta de Ojen (36.14341N 5.59378W) is a good place from which to scan. Just beyond here, the beautiful cork-oak woodlands are well worth spending time in, although they are mostly fenced off, making it very difficult to get good views of the birds. There is a footpath into the woods (signposted to San Carlos del Tiradero) from a lay-by at (36.16317N 5.58219W) but I found this less productive than walking the 2km or so back along the road. Species such as Bonelli's Warbler, Firecrest, Short-toed Treecreeper, Crested Tit, Great Spotted Woodpecker and especially Hawfinch are all numerous here. The main attraction, however, is Iberian Chiff-chaff which has a completely different song from 'our' birds. I transcribed it as *'chiff-chiff-chiff, swit-wit'*, lacking the usual bouncing rhythm and dropping in pitch at the end. In May 2009 I was disappointed to find only one singing bird, next to where the footpath begins. I should point out that the road through the Ojen Valley, beyond the first 6km, is dreadful. Other species I've seen en route include Bee-eater, Golden Oriole, Wryneck, Woodchat Shrike, Subalpine Warbler, Melodious Warbler, Tawny Pipit, Short-toed Lark and Cirl Bunting.

In common with several other birders I have found the nearby Barbate estuary to be a little disappointing although the gulls and terns here will sometimes include Audouin's, Mediterranean and Caspian Tern. In 2004 some Bald Ibis were released in the Sierra de Retin and since then have sometimes been seen around the estuary and by the coast road. Little Swifts have at least attempted to breed amongst the buildings in the port of Barbate.

Gibraltar to Tarifa

Attraction

This stretch of coastline is famous for the spectacular bird-of-prey migrations which can be seen here every spring and autumn. Counts suggest that this area gets almost twice as many migrating raptors as the even more famous Bosphorus at Istanbul. This difference is due largely to the 100,000 extra Honey Buzzards which occur here but Gibraltar also gets 5 times as many Short-toed Eagles, 10 times as many Egyptian Vultures and 30 times more Booted Eagles (based on autumn figures). Black Kites, Sparrowhawks, Kestrels, Montagu's Harrriers and Griffon Vultures also occur in much greater numbers here compared with Istanbul. As an added bonus, these viewpoints have also recently had regular sightings of Ruppell's Vultures. There are impressive migrations of seabirds and passerines too.

Getting there

All the viewing points can be found easily from the main E5/N-340 road between Marbella and Tarifa. There is currently free access between Gibraltar and Spain although you may have to queue to get through customs.

Notes

1. Raptor migration at Gibraltar is most impressive if there is a westerly wind. In spring this can produce the unforgettable spectacle of numbers of eagles and vultures struggling across the sea from Morocco, arriving at Gibraltar almost at sea-level, then soaring up over the Rock. The southern tip of the rock, the Punta de Europa is the best spot for sea-watching (there's an observation hut there) but you get better views of the raptors by being a little higher, at 'Jew's Gate' or on the 'Mediterranean Steps'. These can be found by following signs to the 'Upper Rock', past the Rock Hotel to the first car-park after the toll-booth (36.12088N 5.34588W). Next to the car-park is an information centre manned by volunteers from the Gibraltar Ornithological Society – hence a great place to find out what's about. Beside this are some steps leading to a nature-trail around the south-facing cliffs. From here you would get magnificent views of migrating raptors and stand a chance of seeing Barbary Partridge. The bushy hillside is also excellent for migrant passerines.

2. Even without customs delays, Gibraltar can be a motorist's nightmare; there are simply too many cars on its steep narrow streets. To see similar birds without the potential hassle, you could visit Punta Carnera on the opposite side of Algeciras Bay. To get here, drive straight through Algeciras on the main road until, just as you emerge from the town, look for a roundabout (36.11019N 5.45786W) with a turn-off to the south signposted to Getares. Follow this road to another roundabout, turn right and follow the road around the coast until, just past the left turn to the lighthouse, you find a pull-in on the left. Watch from here for migrating raptors, especially during westerlies.

3. On most days, Tarifa gets larger numbers of raptors than Gibraltar since it is actually closer to Morocco and because the prevailing easterlies (levanters) blow them towards the Atlantic. Such birds can be conveniently viewed from the Mirador de Estrecho (Viewpoint of the Straits), next to the main road, about 7km east of Tarifa (36.05400N 5.55041W). The large, well-signposted car-park has a cafe for endless refreshments while you watch the raptors but you may not appreciate the curiosity of the endless stream of tourists who stop here. A quieter, and better, spot can be found by taking a track to the right about 100 metres along the road towards Tarifa (36.05421N 5.55188W). Follow this to a signposted observatory (sometimes called Cazalla or Cigueña Negra), complete with seats and tables, which offers even better views, especially to the West. This is one of the sites that has most regularly had Ruppell's Vulture. Another is at El Algarrobo which is best approached by driving west from

Tarifa to Gibralter

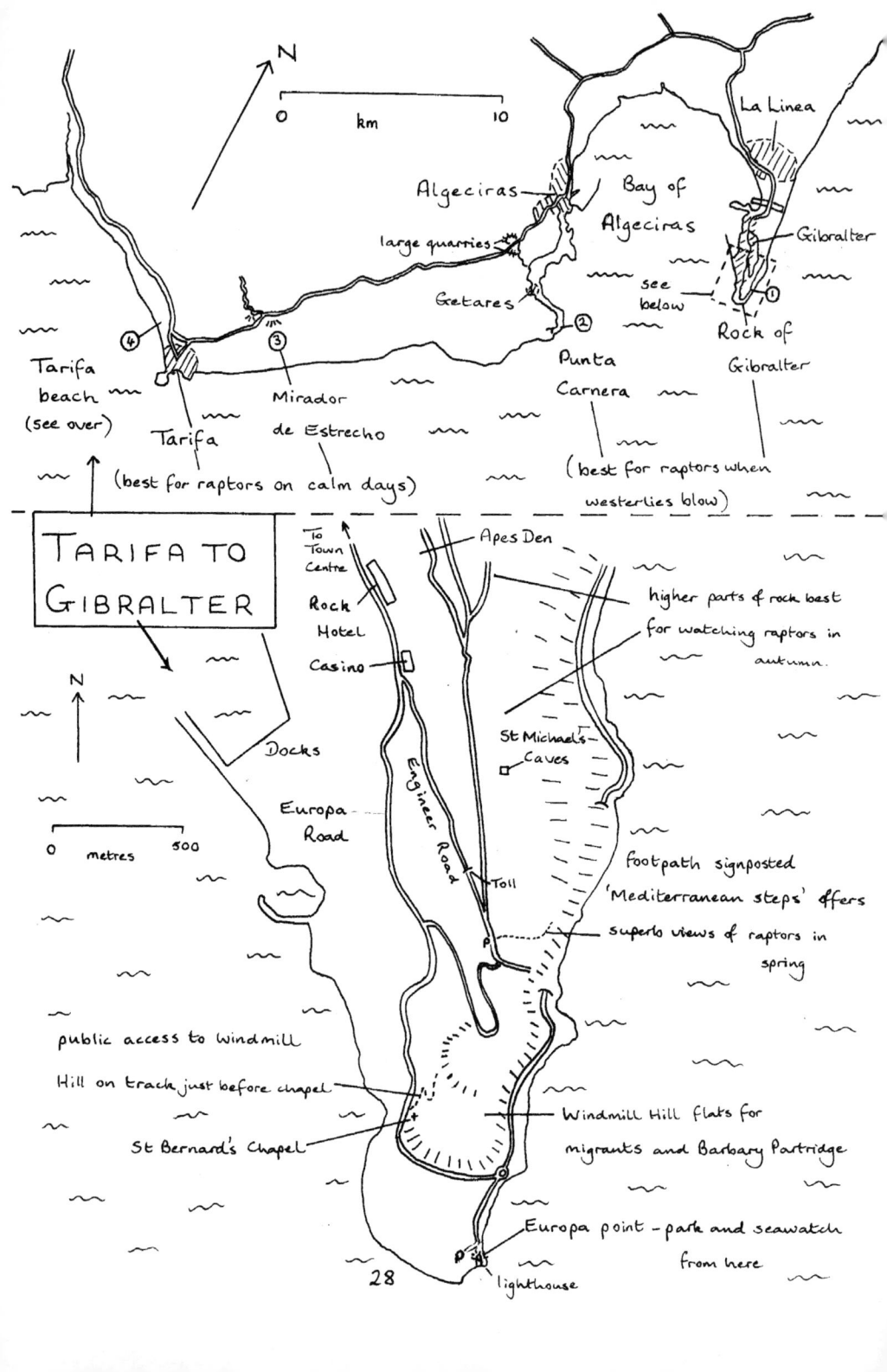

N
0 km 10

La Linea
Algeciras
Bay of Algeciras
large quarries
Gibralter
see below
Rock of Gibralter
Getares
② Punta Carnera
④ Tarifa beach (see over)
③ Mirador de Estrecho
Tarifa (best for raptors on calm days)
(best for raptors when westerlies blow)

N
0 metres 500

To Town Centre
Rock Hotel
Casino
Docks
Europa Road
Engineer Road
Toll
Apes Den
higher parts of rock best for watching raptors in autumn.
St Michael's Caves
footpath signposted 'Mediterranean steps' offers superb views of raptors in spring

public access to Windmill Hill on track just before chapel
St Bernard's Chapel
Windmill Hill flats for migrants and Barbary Partridge
Europa point - park and seawatch from here
lighthouse

28

Algeciras and turning off to the right at km 99.1 on a signposted track (36.08754N 5.49070W). Follow this track to the observation hut.

4. Raptors can also be watched from Tarifa beach but, at sea-level, you don't get such good views. However, the beach is always worth a visit for its gulls and waders. Audouin's and Mediterranean Gulls are regular and rarer species such as Lesser Crested Tern or Ring-billed Gull often linger here. To get there, take the westernmost road into Tarifa and turn right at the first roundabout (36.02620N 5.61185W), before the Mercadona supermarket. This street winds towards the coast, past a new football stadium to a car park (36.02430N 5.61661W). Walk north from there along the boardwalk checking the gulls and waders on the beach to the left and the larks (including Calandras, especially in winter) in the dunes to the right.

The best time for raptor migration is probably late-March to mid-April when the more exciting eagles and vultures reach their peak numbers. An earlier visit would produce mainly Black Kites, whilst a watch in May would be best for the Honey Buzzards. In autumn, late September or early October should give the greatest variety, although the Moroccan side would probably provide better views.

Ronda and the Sierra de Grazalema

Attraction

Ronda itself sits spectacularly above steep cliffs on which Lesser Kestrels and Peregrine Falcons breed. By driving around through the nearby mountain ranges you should see numerous other raptors, including Bonelli's Eagle, plus Black Wheatear, Rock Sparrow, Chough, Rock Bunting and, at least in winter, Alpine Accentor. Eagle Owl and White-rumped Swift are also possible.

Getting there

Ronda is only about 60km North of Marbella. To get there from Malaga airport, follow the N340 towards Cadiz then turn North on the A-397.

Notes

1. The cliffs at Ronda can be easily viewed from the bridge over the famous gorge, from a quieter area of gardens just North of the bull-ring, or from the grounds of the Hotel Reina Victoria a little further North. From any of these viewpoints you should see Pallid Swift, Alpine Swift, Crag Martin and Lesser Kestrel. Peregrines and Rock Buntings are most likely to be seen from the Gardens, whilst Chough and Rock Sparrow particularly frequent the gorge. Raven, Booted Eagle and distant Griffon and Egyptian Vultures are also possible and Roger Smith had an Alpine Accentor by the bridge in April 2005.

2. Any of the mountain roads around Ronda could produce good birds. A particularly good spot is the Puerto de los Palomas (36.80162N 5.38199W). A winter visit here produced 8 Ring Ousel, 7 Alpine Accentors, 10+ Rock Buntings, 3 Black Wheatear, 3 Blue Rock Thrush, 3 Griffons, 6 Red-billed Chough, 3 Dartford Warblers and a Woodlark. At least in winter, the Alpine Accentors and Rock Buntings can be seen at ridiculously close range in the car-park. Summer is less productive though; in May 2009 I had Chough, Peregrine, Griffon Vultures and Bonelli's Warbler; Rock Thrush is regularly seen here too.

3. North of the summit, a gorge called Gargante Verde is a traditional Bonelli's Eagle site though in 2009 I couldn't confirm they were still there. There is a well-marked path to this site but it starts at a gate where there is a sign saying 'no entry without authorization from the visitor centre in El Bosque (over an hour's drive away). If you have the necessary permit you can reach this spot by driving north from the pass as far as 'new km 10' (there are old km posts too, numbered in the other direction!) where there is a car park (36.80818N 5.39235W) by the gate. Alternatively the same area can also be viewed, more distantly but more comprehensively, from the Mirador just up the road at 'old km 14' (36.80106N 5.38923W). The light is better in the mornings.

The map opposite shows more areas for birds in these mountains. White-rumped Swift could be chanced upon from any of these places, including Ronda itself. A more specific nesting site for this species was described as follows in a trip report by M. Jonassohn (per Joakim Djerf): 'in a cleft 3.0 km W of the bridge over Rio Guadiaro (just NW of Ronda) along the A-376'.

RONDA and SIERRA DE GRAZALEMA

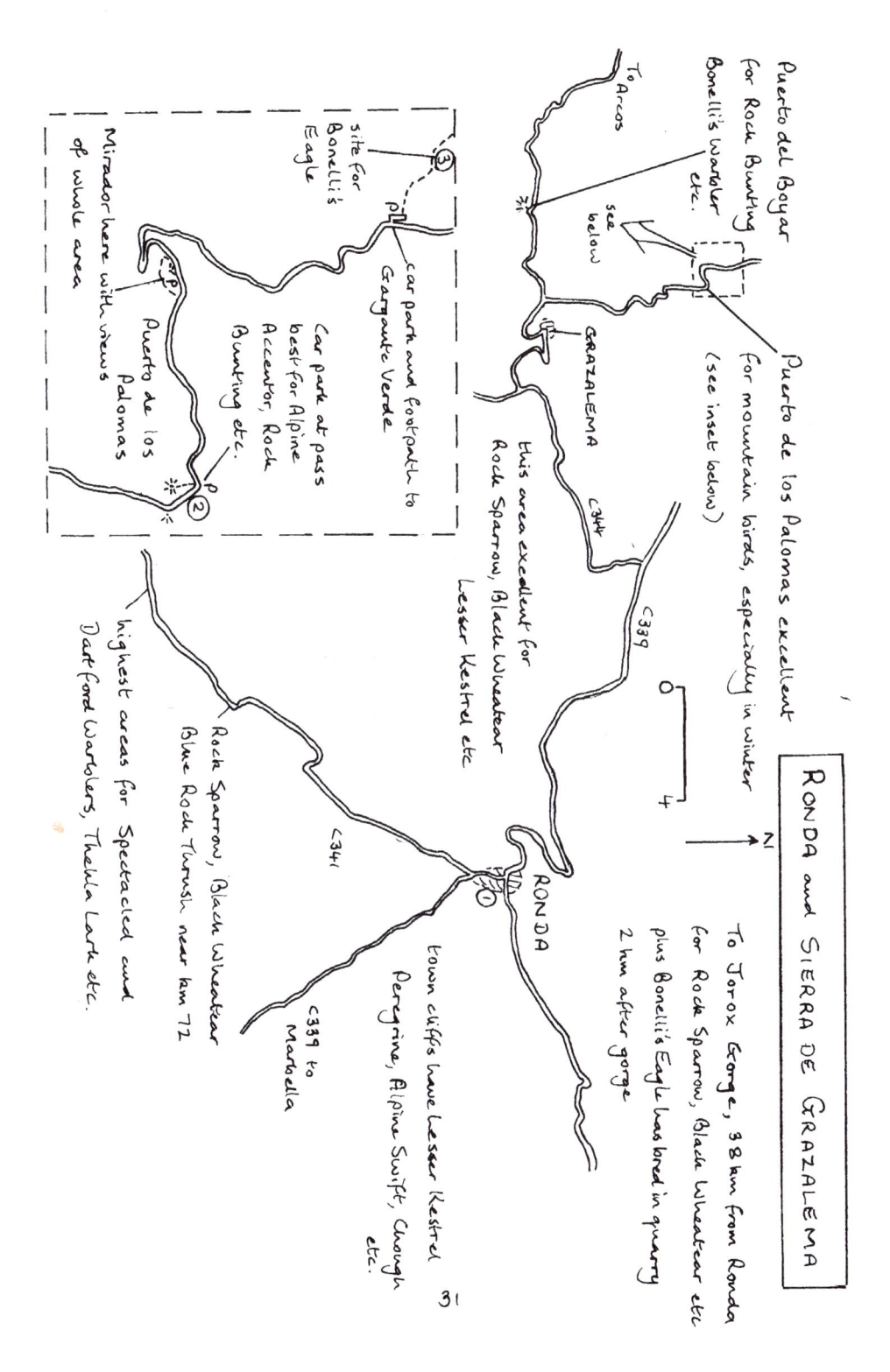

Puerto del Boyar for Rock Bunting, Bonelli's Warbler etc.

Puerto de los Palomas excellent for mountain birds, especially in winter (see inset below)

To Arcos

GRAZALEMA — C344

site for Bonelli's Eagle

car park and footpath to Garganta Verde

Car park at pass best for Alpine Accentor, Rock Bunting etc.

Puerto de los Palomas

Mirador here with views of whole area

this area excellent for Rock Sparrow, Black Wheatear, Lesser Kestrel etc.

C339

To Jorox Gorge, 38 km from Ronda for Rock Sparrow, Black Wheatear etc plus Bonelli's Eagle has bred in quarry 2 km after gorge

N →

RONDA

C339 to Marbella

town cliffs have Lesser Kestrel, Peregrine, Alpine Swift, Chough etc.

C341

Rock Sparrow, Black Wheatear, Blue Rock Thrush near km 72

highest areas for Spectacled and Dartford Warblers, Thekla Lark etc.

31

Lagunas de Espera

Attraction

Tucked away in a quiet bit of countryside, this is a delightful spot with 3 attractive lakes. White-headed Duck and Purple Gallinule should be easy to find. I had Red-knobbed Coot and Little Bittern as well and Marbled Duck and Ferruginous Duck also occur here. However, you get much better views at Laguna de Medina, for example.

Getting there

The village of Espera is 13 km north of Arcos de la Frontera. At the north end of Espera, take the CA-6100 west towards Las Cabezas. Follow this road for almost 3km to a turn-off (36.88238N 5.82885W) marked with a sign for the nature reserve ('Reserva Natural Complejo Endorreico de España'). Follow the rather bumpy road south for 1.5 km then turn right and drive west for a further 3.1 km until the first lake appears on your left. Park by the visitor centre (36.87196N 5.85932W).

Notes

1. The first lake (Laguna de Hondilla) is almost completely overgrown with willows etc. but some open water can still be seen by walking around to the back of the visitor centre. By driving about 500m further on (to 36.87258N 5.86342W) and viewing from the road you will be closer to the lake but will have to be content with seeing birds flying over. We saw a selection of wildfowl, including Red-crested Pochard, and heard Black-necked Grebe.

2. About 200m further along the road is a footpath to the left, marked with a gate and an information board about the reserve. Walk south from here for 300 metres to an observation hut on the left, overlooking the next pool (Laguna Salada de Zorrilla). This is probably the best of several vantage points. This is a bigger, more open, lake with hundreds of Coot and lots more ducks and grebes. Amongst them on my visit were 3 White-headed Duck, at least 4 Black-necked Grebe and plenty of Red-crested Pochard.

3. The third pool (Laguna Dulce de Zorrilla) is reached by continuing to walk south on the same path for a further 1400 metres. The walk takes you through pleasant countryside with birds such as Red-legged Partridge (many), Pheasant and (Iberian) Green Woodpecker. The number of partridge may account for the regular sightings here of Bonelli's Eagle (= 'Partridge Eagle' in Spanish). The lake is attractively reed-fringed and on my visit had at least one Red-knobbed Coot and more Black-necked Grebes and Red-crested Pochard. I also heard Purple Gallinule and Little Bittern.

LAGUNAS de ESPERA

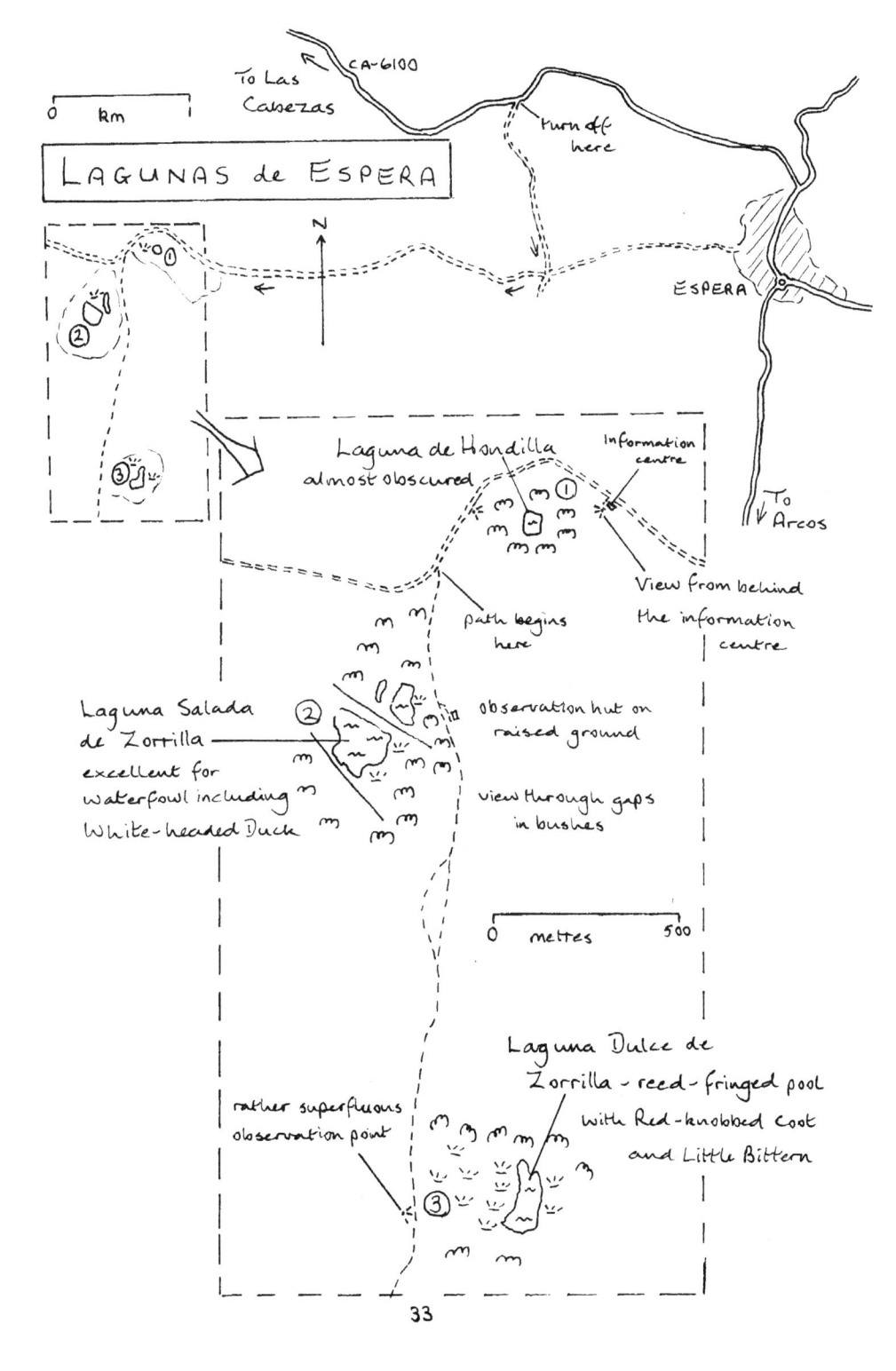

To Las Cabezas
CA-6100
Turn off here
ESPERA
To Arcos

Laguna de Hondilla almost obscured
Information centre
View from behind the information centre
path begins here
observation hut on raised ground
view through gaps in bushes

Laguna Salada de Zorrilla — excellent for waterfowl including White-headed Duck

rather superfluous observation point

Laguna Dulce de Zorrilla — reed-fringed pool with Red-knobbed Coot and Little Bittern

Via Verde near Coripe

(including the Peñon de Zaframagon)

Attraction

The Via Verde is an old railway line that has been converted into a footpath/cycle track. It follows an attractive valley and passes two particularly good sites for birds: the rock at Peñon de Zaframagon has a spectacular colony of Griffon Vultures and a breeding pair of Bonelli's Eagle and another cliff has Bonelli's Eagle and Eagle Owl visible from the track.

Getting there

Both sites can be accessed from Coripe which is due south of Moron de la Frontera on the A-8127. Alternatively, you can drive closer to Zaframagon by taking a minor road north from the A-384 just west of Olvera.

Notes

1. The Peñon de Zaframagon is an impressive rock with a colony of about 100 pairs of Griffon Vultures and a pair of Bonelli's Eagles. There's a visitor centre here with CCTV facilities that give live views of the breeding raptors; if they don't have a live camera on the eagles they can at least show you previously filmed footage of them. One way to get there is to park at Coripe station (36.96501N 5.42985W) and walk east along the Via Verde for 5km to the visitor centre. We did this in December 2008 and enjoyed birds such as Hawfinch and Cirl Bunting en route. Alternatively, you can get closer by car by turning north off the A-384 about 5km west of Olvera (at 36.94362N 5.306364W) signposted to La Muela. After 2.5km the road bends sharply left (at 36.954175N 5.33144W) but take the bumpy track straight on under the railway arches ahead of you. Follow this for 4.1 km to the Cortijo de Zaframagon where you'll be able to see the rock from the opposite side to the visitor centre (which is about a 2.3 km walk away, along the Via Verde).

2. A better place to see Bonelli's Eagle is further west along the Via Verde. To get there, take the A-8127 road towards Montellano from just north of Coripe and, after just over 3km, turn south from this road (at 36.97691N 5.47359W) towards Puerto Serrano. Drive a further 3.1 km and park where this road crosses the Via Verde (at 36.94933N 5.47535W). Walk west from here along the Via Verde and then, after going through a tunnel, you'll see the rock across the valley to your left. In May 2009 the Bonelli's Eagle nest was obvious on the rock, complete with perched adult and flapping white chick. I'm told it is also possible to see Eagle Owl from here at its daytime roost but I couldn't find it.

VIA VERDE NEAR CORIPE

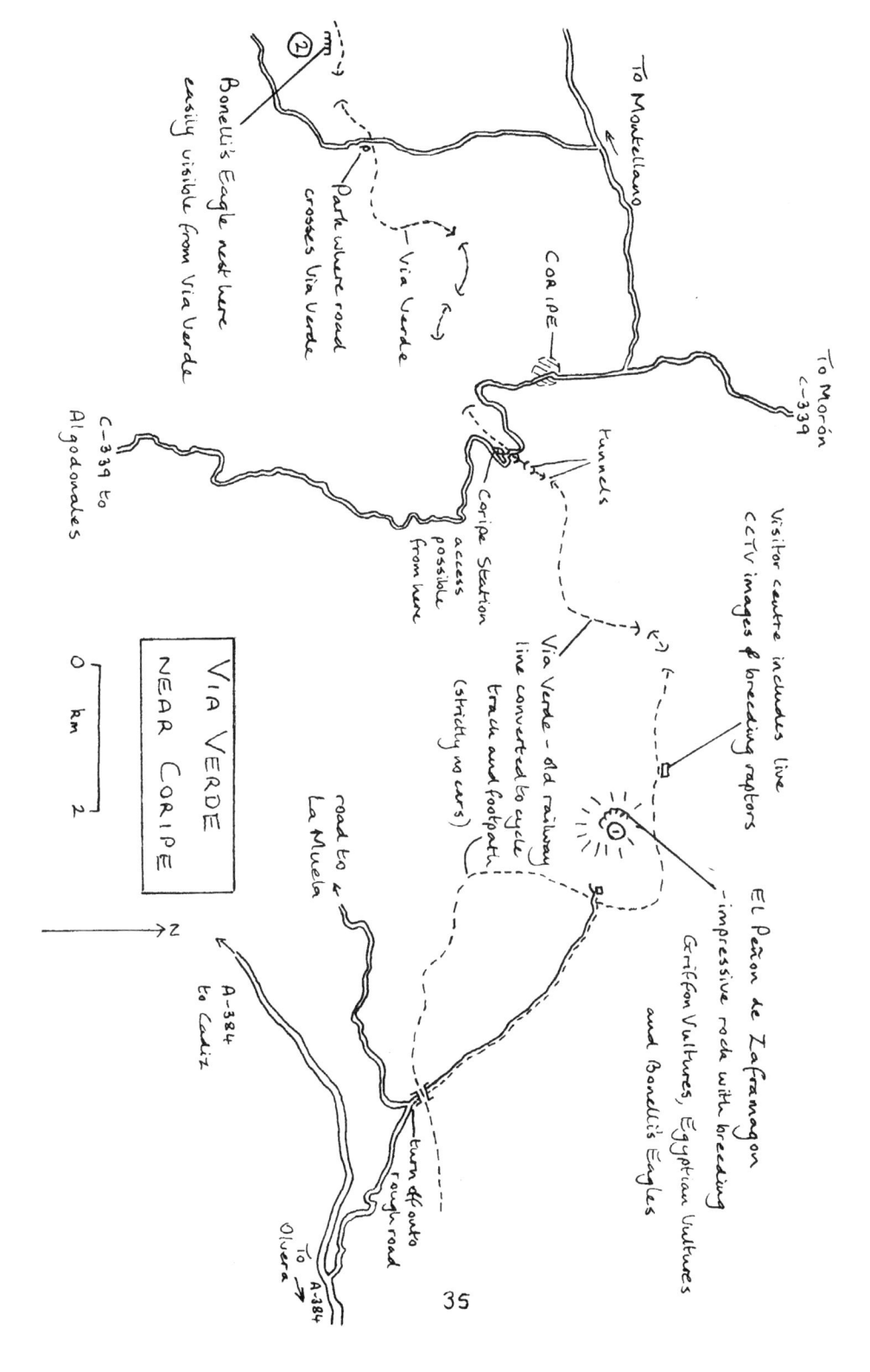

0 km 2

→ N

TO Montellano

TO Morón
C-339

CORIPE

C-339 to Algodonales

A-384 to Cadiz

TO Olvera
A-384

- Bonelli's Eagle nest here easily visible from Via Verde
- Park where road crosses Via Verde
- Via Verde
- Coripe Station access possible from here
- Tunnels
- Via Verde — old railway line converted to cycle track and footpath (strictly no cars)
- road to La Muela
- turn off onto rough road
- Visitor centre includes live CCTV images of breeding raptors
- El Peñon de Zaframagon — impressive rock with breeding Griffon Vultures, Egyptian Vultures and Bonelli's Eagles

35

La Lantejuela

Attraction

This is one of the few places in Andalucia where Great Bustards and Black-bellied Sandgrouse can still be seen, at least in winter. Nearby are several seasonal lagoons that can be good for wildfowl, including White-headed Duck; Black-shouldered Kites and Rollers are found here too.

Getting there

Lantejuela is about 70 km due east of Sevilla. Take the A-92 from Sevilla towards Malaga, then turn north on the A-364 through Marchena towards Ecija. Just after Marchena, turn right, signposted to Lantejuela, about 18 km to the east.

Notes

1. The bustard plains are south of town. Take the A-407 towards Osuna and, just 1km after leaving the last buildings in Lantejuela, look for a rough track on the right (37.33961N 5.21114W). Take this track, if its not too rough, and scan the slopes to the west for bustards (between the road and distant white house). We had a rather distant group of about a dozen birds in December 2008 when there were also Stone Curlews and flocks of Calandra Larks by the track. This area is good for Black-shouldered Kite; we had two by the main road on the edge of town and another at site 4 (see below).

2. Alternatively, turn west from the main road on a better track, 2.8 km south of town (at 37.32595N 5.20096W). From here you can see the same slopes but from even greater distances. However, the track is worth taking anyway, as it takes you through open country which is good for sandgrouse (both species are possible). There's a round trip you can do, as far as the railway line, that covers lots of suitable habitat.

3. Due east of La Lantejuela are some seasonal lagoons which, if flooded, are good for wildfowl and flamingoes in winter and waders during passage. White-headed Ducks are regularly seen and both Marbled Duck and Red-knobbed Coot have been recorded too. The easiest pools to access are between 2 and 4 km along the road to El Rubio (east of La Lantejuela). Beyond here (10 km from town) you reach a crossroads with the A-351; further lagoons may be found along this road too, 5km north and south from here.

4. Another lagoon, smaller but more permanent, is found on the outskirts of La Lantejuela itself. It looks like an old sewage farm. There are a couple of currently makeshift, hides giving terrific views of the hundreds of wintering wildfowl, including regular White-headed Duck. However, it is situated behind a gated entrance so you need to get permission to visit there. This can be arranged in advance by writing to info@birdingsevilla.com, a tourist agency that can also arrange for a guide to show you the bustards and sandgrouse. The lagoon is located by finding the Calle de la Cañada de la Laguna, a road which runs north from a bar in the centre of town (at 37.35616N 5.22245W). The entrance is 800 metres down that road at 37°21'46.02"N 5°13'35.28"W. On our visit in December 2008, we had Marsh Harrier and Black-shouldered Kite here too.

Our best chance of conserving birds like Great Bustard is if the locals can see an economic benefit in ensuring their survival. So why not stop for a drink, an ice-cream or a meal in places like La Lantejuela and make it known you are there to see the birds.

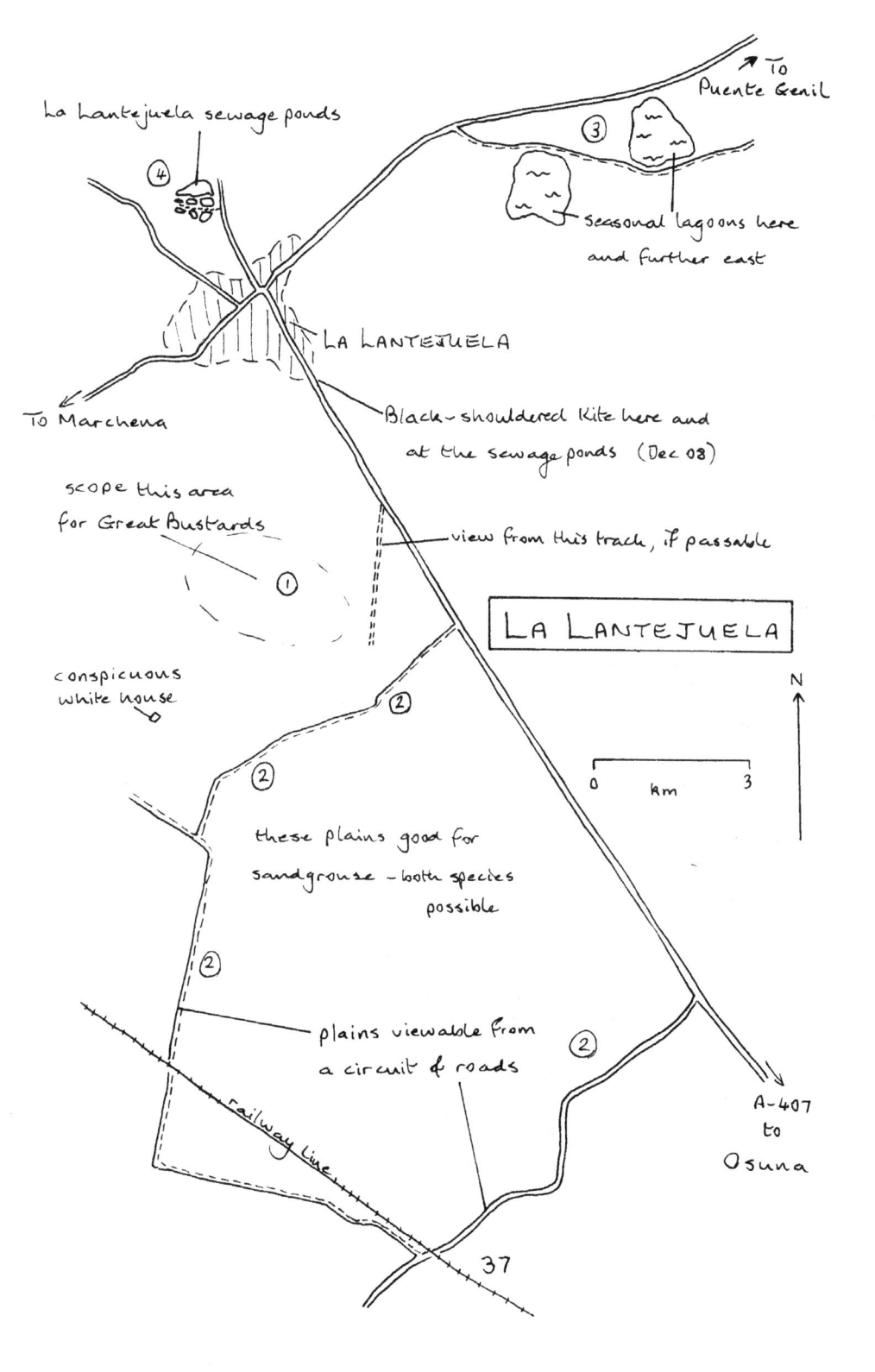

La Lantejuela sewage ponds ④

③

seasonal lagoons here and further east

→ To Puente Genil

To Marchena ←

LA LANTEJUELA

Black-shouldered Kite here and at the sewage ponds (Dec 08)

scope this area for Great Bustards ①

view from this track, if passable

conspicuous white house

LA LANTEJUELA

N ↑

0 — 3 km

②
②
these plains good for sandgrouse – both species possible
②
plains viewable from a circuit of roads
②

Railway line

A-407 to Osuna

37

Laguna de Fuente de Piedra and the Teba Gorge

Attraction

Up to 20,000 pairs of Greater Flamingoes breed here in most years; occasionally it is the largest colony in Europe (though the Camargue is usually bigger). There's always a chance of finding a Lesser Flamingo amongst them. Small wetlands created near the visitor centre host a variety of species at close range including Gull-billed Tern, Avocet, Red-crested Pochard and, sometimes White-headed Duck. Of course, all the waterbirds are dependent on the water-levels and, in a bad year, the whole lake can be dry and birdless. The nearby Teba Gorge has been an excellent spot for Bonelli's Eagle but nowadays is useful merely as a site for commoner rocky species such as Black Wheatear, Rock Sparrow and Blue Rock Thrush.

Getting there

The lagoon of Fuente de Piedra is just west of the main Malaga-Sevilla road (A-92), about 20 km north-west of Antequera. If coming from the south, just follow signs into the village of Fuente de Piedra, then keep straight on, through the village, towards Sierra de Yeguas. After rising over the railway line, look for a road to the left to the visitor centre. Laguna Dulce is a roadside lake just East of Campillos. From here, Teba Gorge can be found by turning south on the A-357 towards Ronda. Take the right turn towards Teba after about 10 km, then, after 3.5km, you'll see gorge on the right.

Notes

1. Apart from the thousands of flamingoes, the roads around the lagoon also provide views of Black-winged Stilts, Avocets and Gull-billed Terns and the surrounding areas have Woodchat and Southern Grey Shrikes and Short-toed Larks. Up to 7 Lesser Flamingoes have been counted amongst the flocks of Greaters and at least one pair has attempted to breed.

2. Around the visitor centre are a number of smaller pools which attract some of the birds from the main lake (flamingoes, Gull-billed Terns, stilts and Avocets) but also support a few species of their own including, in May 2009, Red-crested Pochard, White-headed Duck, Stone Curlew, Whiskered Tern and Mediterranean Gull. In other years I've had lots of passage waders here too. These pools can be easily viewed either from footpaths or from excellent hides.

3. We stayed at the campsite (37.12918N 4.73386W) just south of the village of Fuente de Piedra where the birds heard at night included Stone Curlew and Red-necked Nightjar.

4. The Laguna Dulce is well worth at least a brief stop. In the past I've had Black-necked Grebe and Gull-billed Tern here and White-headed Duck is said to have bred but in May 2009 (when most wetlands seemed to have plenty of water) this was completely dry. There's a lay-by here with a car-park and hide – access is from the eastern end of the lay-by (37.04816N 4.83116W).

5. Teba Gorge can be viewed from the bridge (36.98091N 4.88109W) or by walking along the gorge bottom. It seems likely that Bonelli's Eagles no longer breed here but you should still see most of the birds of rocky areas such as Red-billed Chough, Alpine Swift, Crag Martin, Rock Bunting, Blue Rock Thrush, Black Wheatear and Rock Sparrow. The map also shows a public observation point nearby (36.96721N 4.84726W) for viewing raptors; this looks up at a colony of Griffon and Egyptian Vultures; information signs suggest that Bonelli's Eagles are sometimes seen here too.

Laguna de Fuente de Piedra and the Teba Gorge

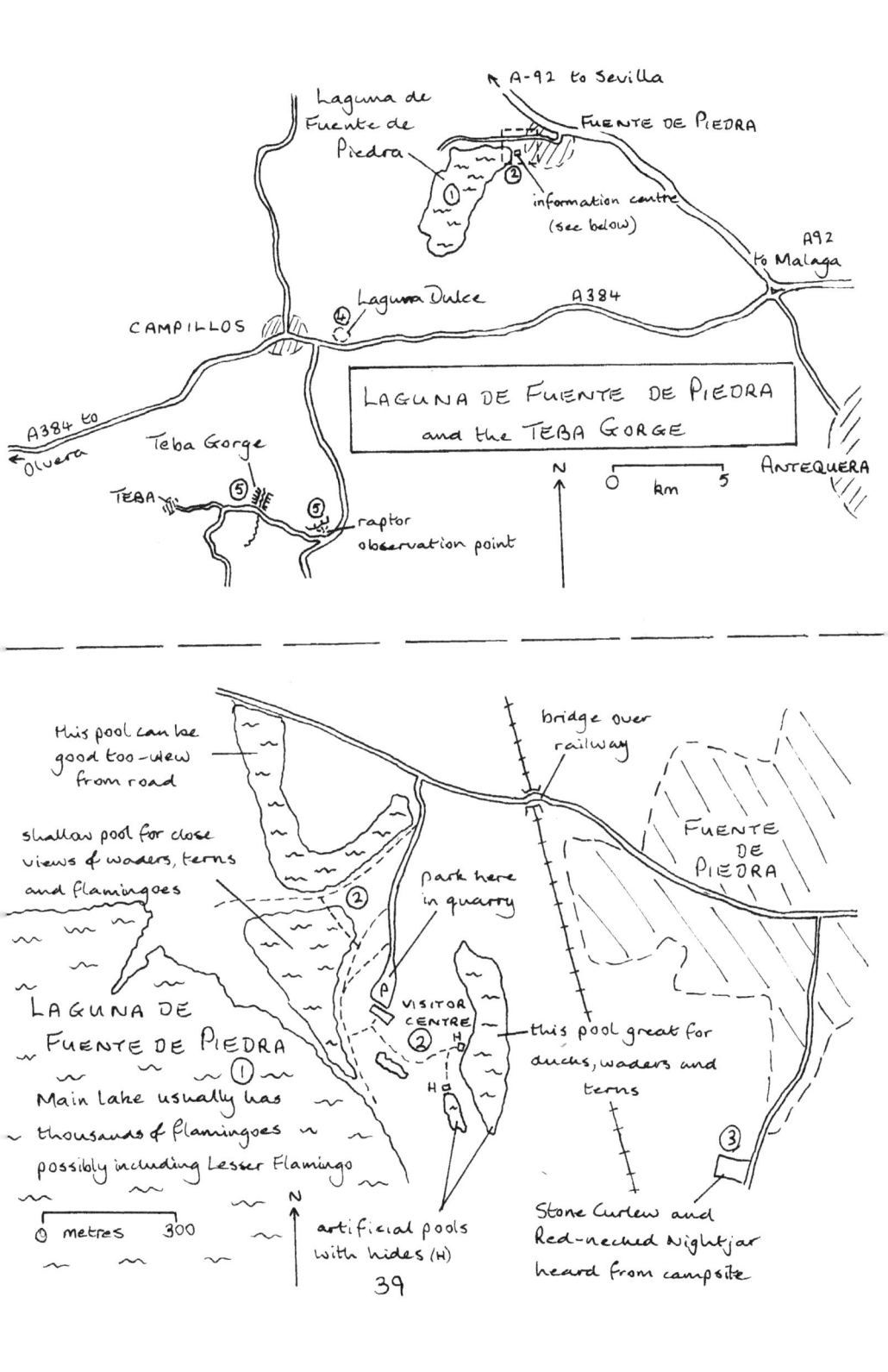

Map 1 (top):
- A-92 to Sevilla
- Fuente de Piedra
- Laguna de Fuente de Piedra ①
- ② information centre (see below)
- A92 to Malaga
- Laguna Dulce ④
- A384
- Campillos
- A384 to Olvera
- Teba Gorge
- Teba ⑤
- ⑤ raptor observation point
- Antequera
- N, 0 — 5 km

Map 2 (bottom): **Laguna de Fuente de Piedra**

- This pool can be good too — view from road
- Shallow pool for close views of waders, terns and flamingoes
- bridge over railway
- park here in quarry
- Fuente de Piedra
- Visitor Centre ②
- this pool great for ducks, waders and terns
- ① Main lake usually has thousands of flamingoes possibly including Lesser Flamingo
- ③ Stone Curlew and Red-necked Nightjar heard from campsite
- artificial pools with hides (H)
- 0 — 300 metres
- N

39

Laguna de Zonar and Laguna de Rincon

Attraction

In recent years there has been plenty of water at many sites in Andalucia so these lakes have been less significant but, when most of Andalucia was dry, they provided almost the last refuge for White-headed Ducks. If ever this species becomes elusive again, this should be the best bet as a last resort. These two lakes are the best of 8 wetlands which together make up a reserve called the 'Wetlands South of Cordoba'. Of the other sites, Amarga can also be good for White-headed Duck and the Embalse de Malpassillo (a reservoir) is perhaps the best of these areas for Purple Gallinule. Red-knobbed Coot has been introduced to this area too.

Getting there

The Laguna de Zonar (pronounced like Sonya) can be seen from the C329 about 4 km SW of Aguilar. To get to Rincon you must take the N33 1 SE from Aguilar, then follow the first road to the right towards Moriles. After about 5km, look for a track to the right (37.46435N 4.61974W) with a signpost to the nature reserve. Follow this track for 900 metres to find the lake on your left.

Notes

1. The lake can be viewed from a public hide near the southern shore. To get, there, take the old road just east of where the A-304 goes over a railway line. This leads to a car park and visitor centre (37.47787N 4.68751W). If the centre is open you can take a path under the railway line which leads to the hide.

2. To get better views, you should find the track to the east of the lake (from 37.48656N 4.67884W). You can drive along this track, over the railway line, to the northern end of the lake. An early morning visit would be best here to avoid looking into the sun. Please respect the notices and fences asking you not to try to get closer to the lake. Over 100 White-headed Ducks have been seen here in winter but the productivity of the lake was almost destroyed by the introduction of carp. Thankfully, these have now been eradicated and the White-headed Ducks are beginning to return.

3. An observation hide here is not open to the public. Shame.

4. The Laguna de Rincon is remarkably small (village ponds are usually bigger) but exceptionally important when other wetlands dry up. The water surface can be filled with birds, mostly Coot and Mallard but including Black-necked Grebe, Red-crested Pochard and White-headed Duck (up to a dozen females breed here). The waterbirds can be viewed by walking along the edge of the fields to the west of the reserve. The reserve itself is fenced off so the hides are usually inaccessible since the reception centre (37.46143N 4.62891W) is unmanned. Other birds here include Purple Gallinule and the introduced Red-knobbed Coot.

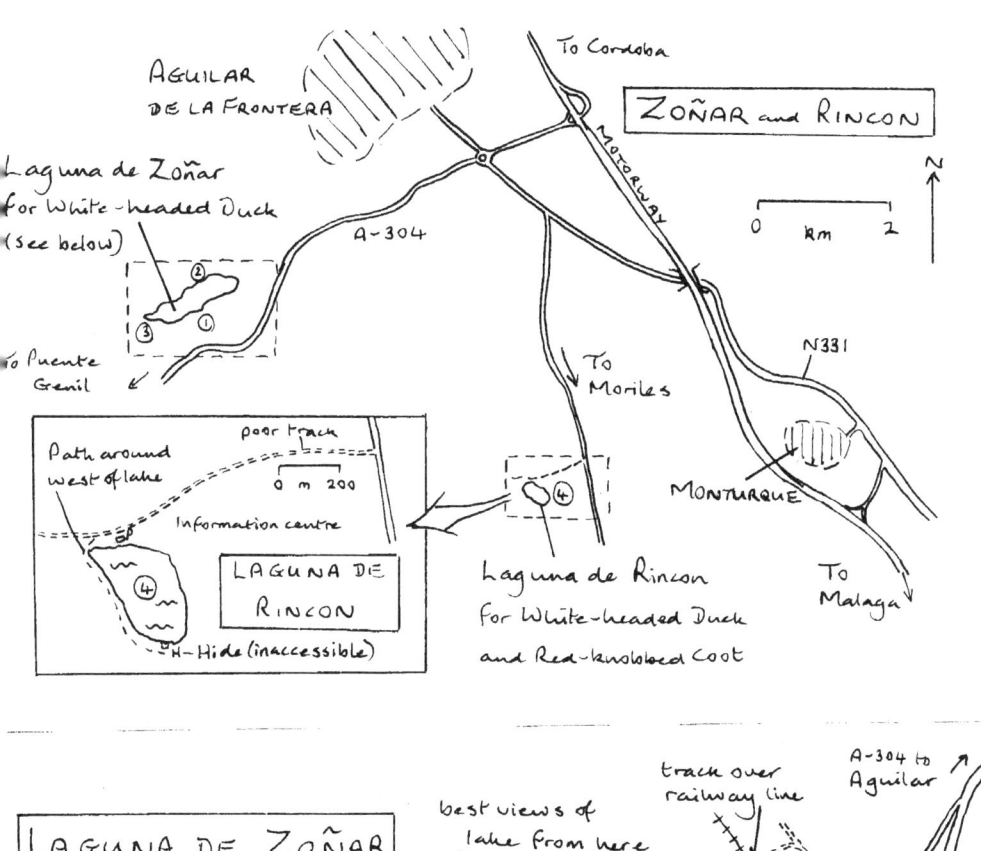

ZOÑAR and RINCON

AGUILAR DE LA FRONTERA

Laguna de Zoñar for White-headed Duck (see below)

To Puente Genil

To Cordoba

A-304

Motorway

0 km 2

N331

To Moriles

MONTURQUE

Laguna de Rincon for White-headed Duck and Red-knobbed Coot

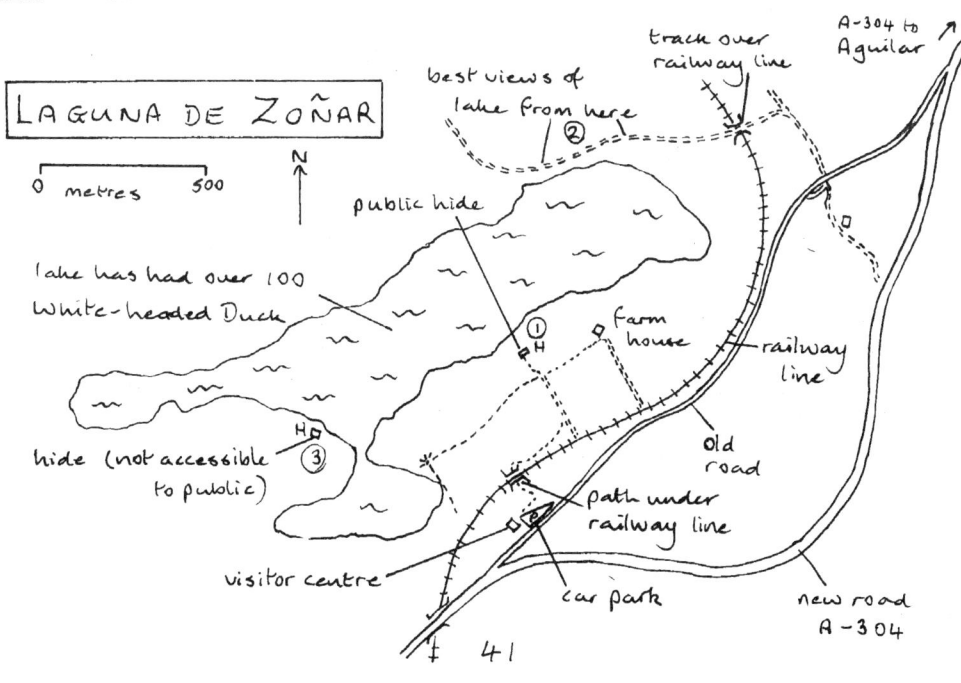

To Malaga

LAGUNA DE RINCON

Path around west of lake
poor track
0 m 200
Information centre
H – Hide (inaccessible)

LAGUNA DE ZOÑAR

0 metres 500

lake has had over 100 White-headed Duck

hide (not accessible to public)

visitor centre

best views of lake from here ②

public hide

farm house

track over railway line

A-304 to Aguilar

railway line

old road

path under railway line

car park

new road A-304

41

Almeria

Attraction

Beyond the seas of plastic greenhouses, the open country of Almeria is home to special birds such as Trumpeter Finch, Bonelli's Eagle and Black-bellied Sandgrouse, though these can all be elusive, as well as Dupont's Lark, Eagle Owl and Little Bustard which are even harder to see. The unobliging nature of these birds, the grimness of both the plastic countryside and the weather (which is frequently either too hot or too windy) means Almeria is not my favourite birding location! In mitigation it offers some very enjoyable birding at wetland sites such as Cañada de las Norias, Roquetas del Mar and Rambla Morales with species such as White-headed Duck, Marbled Duck, Slender-billed Gull and Audouin's Gull being the star attractions.

Getting There

Almeria is 220 km east of Malaga and the best birding areas are shown opposite.

Notes

1. Tucked away amongst all the plastic greenhouses is a terrific wetland called Cañada de Las Norias which offers fantastic views of birds such as White-headed Duck, Black-necked Grebe and, if you're lucky, Marbled Duck (more details on page 47).

2. Along the strip of coast to the west of Roquetas de Mar are the lagoons of the mostly-disused Cerrillos salt pans (or Salinas Vieja). This area attracts a great variety of waterbirds in all seasons, including good numbers of passage waders. It is a particularly good site for flamingoes, Stone Curlews and Lesser-Short-toed Larks. Hundreds of Audouin's Gulls occur in winter, when passerines include Penduline Tit and Bluethroat, and there are often dozens of White-headed Ducks, some of which breed here. It is possible to reach this site by walking west along the beach from Roquetas, then cutting inland after the line of pine trees but it's easier to drive along the northern edge of the saltpans (the road to Almerimar) looking for one of several tracks to the south (eg at 36.71100N 2.66943W) which lead through the pans towards the coast.

3. The Campo de Nijar is another of the areas that is said to be good for Trumpeter Finch and Dupont's Lark. The latest Birdlife figures (for 1996!) suggest 100 pairs of Trumpeter Finch (down from 200) and 50 pairs of Dupont's Lark (down from 150) but I suspect there have been further declines since then. In May 2009 I visited both of the sites near Cuevas de los Ubedas recommended by Garcia and Patterson (2008). I camped overnight 2 km south of the village and walked the plateau at dusk and the main gully from dawn the following morning but, just as on my previous visit in April 1991, I failed to find either species. Remarkably, this time I didn't see a single wheatear, of any species, either; the best birds were Thekla Larks, Red-rumped Swallow, Bee-eater, Little Owl and Red-necked Nightjar. I then tried their site for Dupont's Lark (on the same road but just north of the motorway) and found that their 'low, wide, flat area' was now covered in plastic. Should you wish to try this area for yourself, you can find the signposted road to Cuevas de los Ubedas by turning north from the N-334 at a roundabout just west of Retamar. However, the areas around Cabo de Gata (sites 4 and 6) are probably a better bet for both species.

ALMERIA AREA

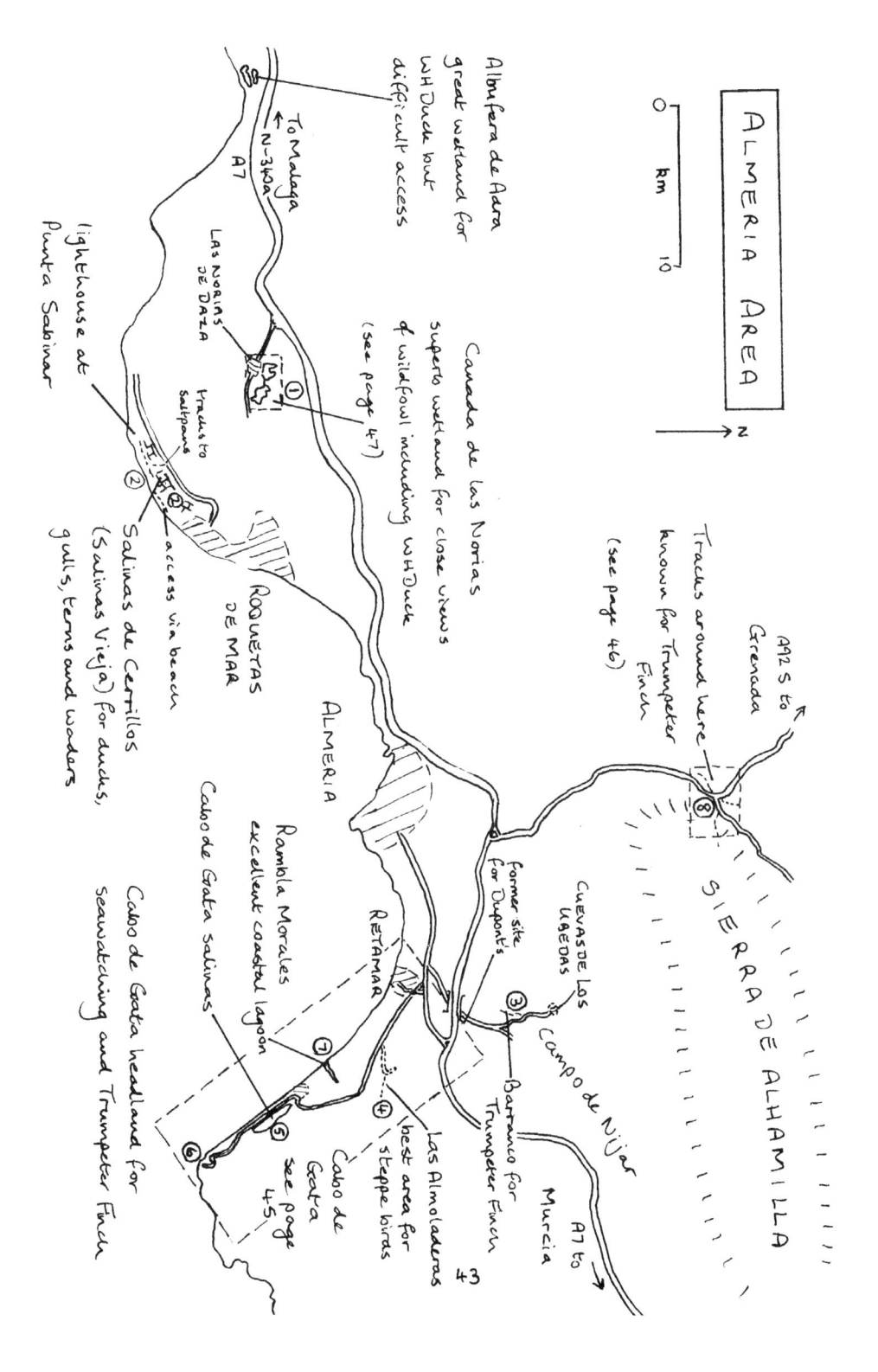

N →

0 — 10 km

Albufera de Adra great wetland for WH Duck but difficult access

To Malaga ← N-340a / A7

LAS NORIAS DE DAZA

Cañada de las Norias superb wetland for close views of wildfowl including WH Duck (see page 47)

① tracks to saltpans

② ROQUETAS DE MAR

Salinas de Cerillos (Salinas Vieja) for ducks, gulls, terns and waders

access via beach

lighthouse at Punta Sabinar

ALMERIA

A92 S to Granada

tracks around here known for Trumpeter Finch (see page 46)

SIERRA DE ALHAMILLA

CUEVAS DE LOS UBEDAS

former site for Dupont's

⑧

Campo de Nijar

A7 to Murcia

③ Barranco for Trumpeter Finch

④ Las Almoladeras best area for steppe birds — see page 45

Cabo de Gata

RETAMAR

Rambla Morales excellent coastal lagoon

⑦

Cabo de Gata Salinas

⑤

⑥ Cabo de Gata headland for seawatching and Trumpeter Finch

43

4. Las Almoladeras is probably the best area for the steppe species in Almeria – look here for birds such as Black-bellied Sandgrouse, Roller, Spectacled Warbler, Stone Curlew and maybe even Little Bustard (though these are few in number and rarely seen). Even more elusive are the Dupont's Larks; J H Johns had a singing bird here in February 2003 but Garcia and Patterson (2008) cast doubt on whether any remain. To get there, turn south from the N-334 towards Retamar then look for a left turn at a roundabout, signposted to Cabo de Gata. Almost 4km from that roundabout there's a road to the right for the Almoladeras Visitor Centre and, almost opposite, a road to the left (36.82762N 2.26582W) which leads to a distant beacon. Follow this road for about a kilometre and park where it bends to the left (36.83026N 2.25681W). There's a track to the right from here that takes you across the best-looking steppe habitat in the area; this is where J H Johns had his Dupont's Lark though Black-bellied Sandgrouse was the best bird I had in May 2009.

5. On my first visit to the saltpans at Salinas de Gata, in April 1991, I found them to be excellent for birds, including about 30 Audouin's Gulls, a Slender-billed Gull, Sandwich and Little Terns, Lesser Short-toed Lark, numerous flamingoes and hundreds of waders. In May 2009, however, they were much less exciting with deep water levels making them suitable only for flamingoes and stilts etc; no doubt they could be different again if the levels dropped. Outside the breeding season this is a good site for hundreds of Audouin's Gulls (especially at the southern end of the pans) and, like the Salinas at Roquetas, there are always good numbers of flamingoes and Lesser Short-toed Larks here. To get here, just keep following signs to Cabo de Gata from Retamar. There's a viewing point at the northern end of the pans and a number of screened hides, or at least observation points, accessible from the road. Don't forget to check the pools closest to the village of La Almadrava at the southern end.

6. The road past the saltpans continues to the lighthouse at the rocky headland. This is a good place to scan for seabirds including Cory's and Balearic Shearwaters, which are regular, and Shags, of the race *aristotelis*, which breed here. Bonelli's Eagles also breed along this rocky coast but Peregrines are rather easier to see. Trip reports suggest this is probably the best site to see Trumpeter Finch; they are said to be 'easy' at least outside the breeding season. They have been seen in the following areas: (i) immediately around the lighthouse car park and nearby buildings, (ii) along the last 2km of road before the lighthouse and (iii) along the road just south of La Almadrava as it rises above the plain. I tried all these sites in May 2009 and didn't see Trumpeter Finch at any of them. Remarkably, this time I didn't see Black Wheatear either; have their numbers crashed or does it just indicate how difficult it is to see ANY songbirds in the strong winds that seem to be a feature of this area?

7. Rambla Morales is a really attractive little wetland just up the coast on the north side of Cabo de Gata village. To get there, just 'follow your nose' to the north end of the village then look for the track along the beach. Although this is a bit sandy in places it should be possible to drive for 1.6 km and park where a river is blocked by the beach (36.7935N 2.25814W). This creates a small lagoon, the Rambla Morales. The seaward end of the lagoon is usually good for waders, gulls and terns including marsh terns and Audouin's Gulls. Unless there has been recent rain, you can also drive inland for at least 600 metres by turning right at the car park to follow a track which passes alongside the lagoon. From here, in May 2009 I had superb views of gulls including Slender-billed and Mediterranean and, at the eastern end of the lagoon, I also had Marbled Duck and White-headed Duck.

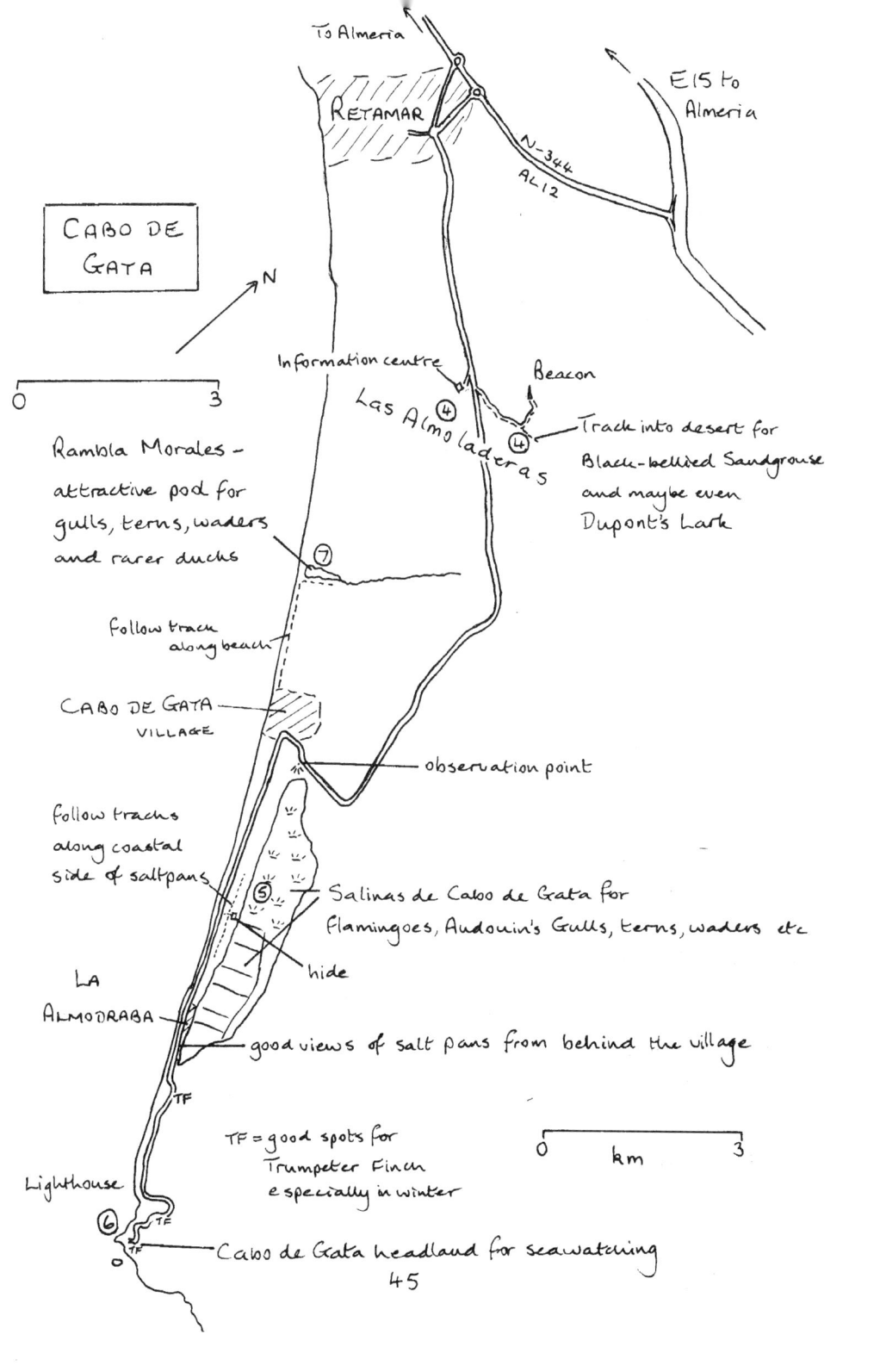

Cabo de Gata

To Almeria

RETAMAR

E15 to Almeria

N-344 / AL12

N

0 — 3

Information centre

Las Almoladeras

Beacon

Track into desert for Black-bellied Sandgrouse and maybe even Dupont's Lark

Rambla Morales - attractive pool for gulls, terns, waders and rarer ducks

Follow track along beach

CABO DE GATA VILLAGE

observation point

follow tracks along coastal side of saltpans

Salinas de Cabo de Gata for Flamingoes, Audouin's Gulls, terns, waders etc

hide

LA ALMODRABA

good views of salt pans from behind the village

TF

TF = good spots for Trumpeter Finch especially in winter

0 — km — 3

Lighthouse

Cabo de Gata headland for seawatching

45

8. The areas around Tabernas look so much like 'real' desert that they have been used as locations for 'Spagetti Westerns' and have attracted Trumpeter Finches normally at home in the Sahara, to stay and breed. However, I have failed to locate them on both my visits. The best known sites for them are by the junction of the A92 and the N-340a. To the north-east of this junction is a deep gully which is said to be accessible from the nearby petrol station (37.01685N 2.44629W). I couldn't see an obvious way of doing that but didn't try too hard because the said gully seemed to be too well vegetated for Trumpeter Finch. Instead I tried the more barren gullies to the south-east but failed to pick up any Trumpeter Finches in very strong winds. Another well-publicised site is on the road leading onto the hills from 'Mini-Hollywood'. Follow signs to this tourist attraction but look for the tarmac road to the left just before the gates (37.02048N 2.43335W). It is possible, with some care, to drive this road for about 15 km to a TV repeater station but it's better to walk the lower gullies to stand a chance of picking up the finches by their calls. Other birds to look for include Crag Martin, Alpine Swift, Black Wheatear, Thekla Lark, Spectacled Warbler, Roller and Black-bellied Sandgrouse.

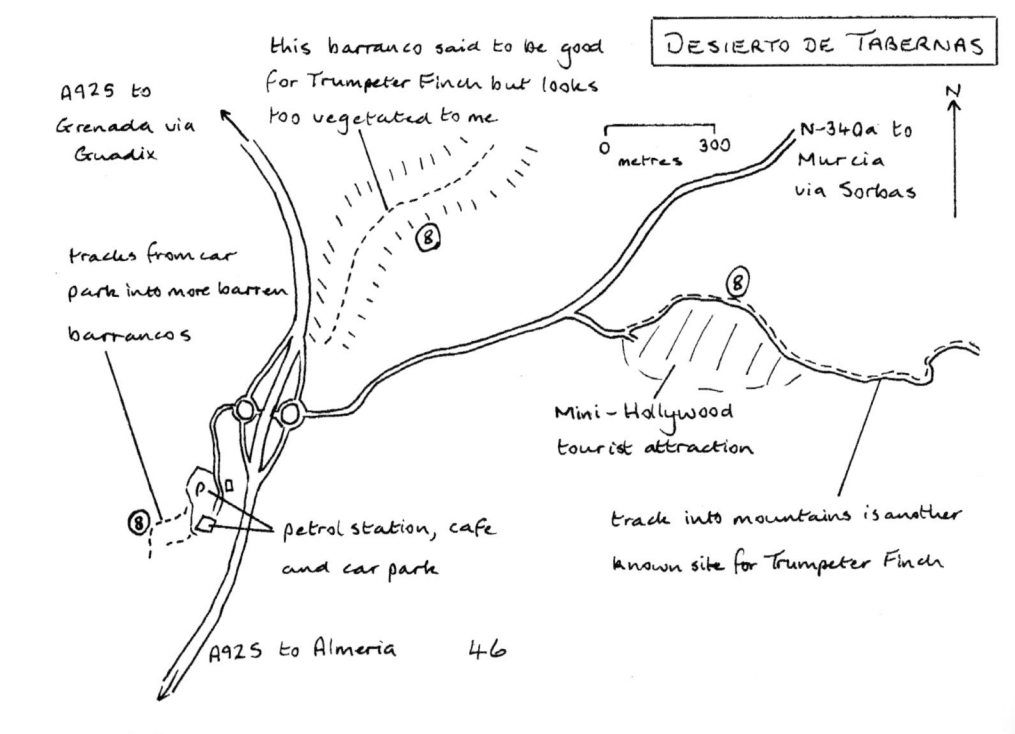

Cañada de las Norias

Attraction

Despite being totally surrounded by miles and miles of plastic sheeting, this is a terrific little wetland, well worth taking the trouble to visit. White-headed Duck is the main attraction, not just because there are so many of them, but also because they give such close views, as do Black-necked Grebes. There's also a heronry which includes Squacco Herons and Night Herons and a chance of Marbled Duck and Little Bittern too. There is another, similar, site the Albufera de Adra, 20km to the west. This has even more White-headed Ducks but is so obscured by fences and reeds (and greenhouses!) that Cañada de las Norias is a much better bet.

Getting there

Turn south from the E-15 motorway, on the A-1050 signposted to Las Norias de Daza. Continue through Las Norias until, just before the 'end of Las Norias' roadsign, you see a minor road to the left (36.75955N 2.73740W). This takes you to one end of the main lake. The rest can be reached by continuing along the A-1050 for a further 1.3 km and turning left just after an obvious white building (and just before the plastics recycling plant).

Notes

1. Driving north, you will see the main lake on your right and another lake, seemingly devoid of birds on the left. Park here (36.76139N 2.737031W) to enjoy remarkably close views of White-headed Duck and Black-necked Grebe right by the road. You can use your vehicle as a hide but if you walk along the road you can use the small lakeside bushes as a shield. Presumably in time these bushes might obscure the views; lets hope some gaps are maintained. Scan from here for other wildfowl (Marbled Duck is regularly seen) and marsh terns (all 3 species have been found).

2. At the east end if the lake you can park by the bridge (36.75818N 2.72283W) and enjoy more fantastic close views of the White-headed Ducks and other wildfowl such as Pochard. The reedy channels to the left of the road are probably the best area for Little Bittern, Penduline Tit and Purple Gallinule.

3. To the right of the road is a pool with some shingle islands at its northern end. This is worth checking too (from 36.76037N 2.721394W) for more ducks and waders which, on my visit, included Red-crested Pochard and Collared Pratincole.

4. Along the northern edge of the main pool are many partly-submerged tamarisk bushes which host a substantial heronry. You can get close to these by parking at a gap in the greenhouses (at 36.76347N 2.72698W) and walking west for 100 metres to the lake edge. Sadly, the height of the nearest tamarisks means the heronry, though very close, is largely obscured; I had to stand on a pile of rubble to get the best views. Most of the birds are Cattle Egrets but there are Squacco and Night Herons amongst them.

CAÑADA DE LAS NORIAS

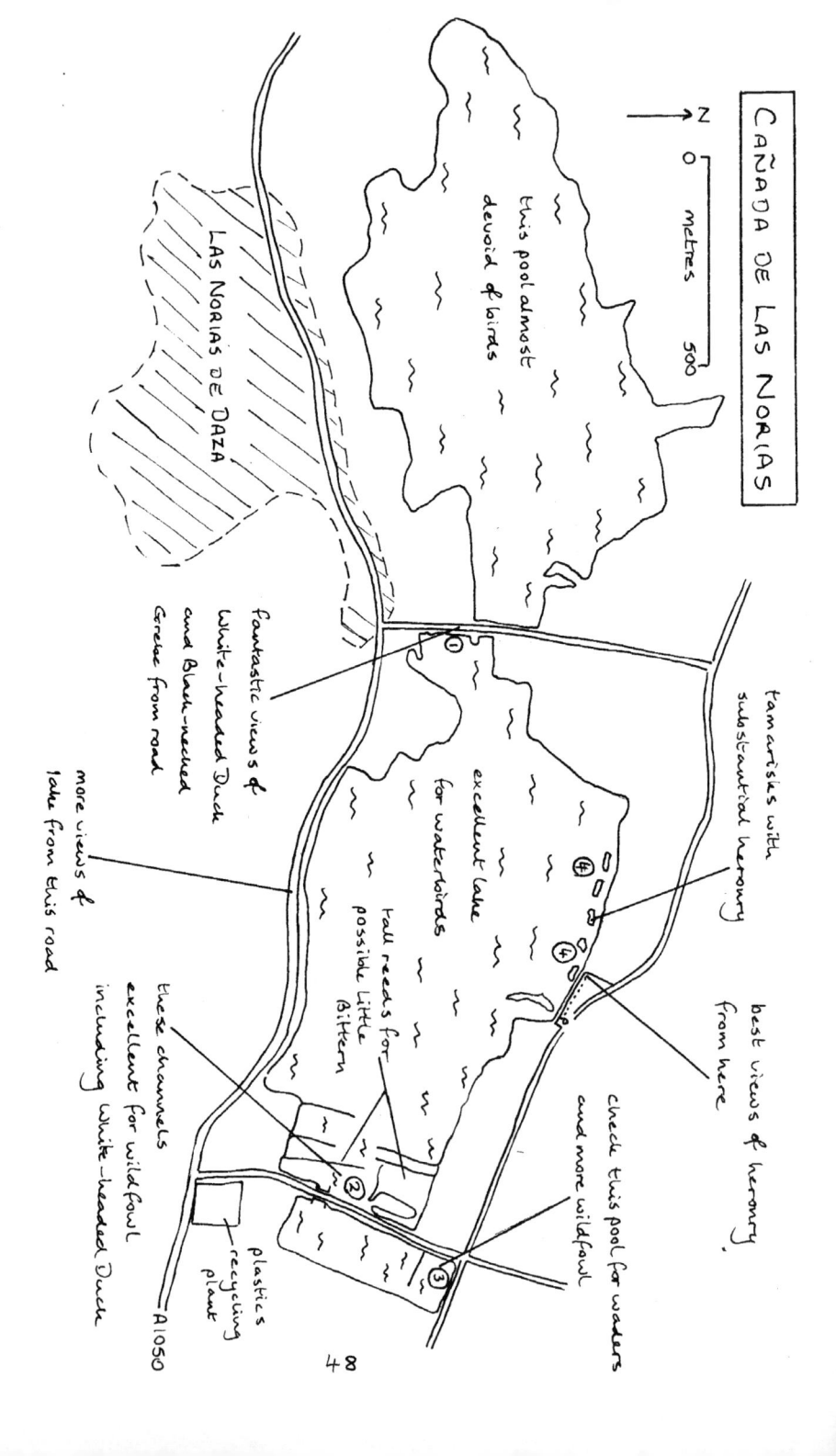

this pool almost devoid of birds

LAS NORIAS DE DAZA

tamarisks with substantial heronry

best views of heronry from here

fantastic views of White-headed Duck and Black-necked Grebe from road

excellent lake for waterbirds

tall reeds for possible Little Bittern

check this pool for waders and more wildfowl

more views of lake from this road

these channels excellent for wildfowl including White-headed Duck

plastics recycling plant

A1050